T0208663

A GUIDE FOR PARENTS
Understanding Policies of
the Public School System in the United States

First Edition
Dr. Elaine Sutton Robertson

authorHOUSE®

AuthorHouse™
1663 Liberty Drive, Suite 200
Bloomington, IN 47403
www.authorhouse.com
Phone: 1-800-839-8640

First published by AuthorHouse 3/4/2009

ISBN: 978-1-4389-3410-5 (sc)
ISBN: 978-1-4389-3410-5

Printed in the United States of America
Bloomington, Indiana

This book is printed on acid-free paper.

Contents

CHAPTER 1
Introduction

The book is a guide for American parents to understand laws that governs the public school system in the United States. Education in the United States is provided mainly by the government, with control and funding from three levels: federal, state and local. School attendance is mandatory from elementary to secondary level. The ages for compulsory education vary by state, beginning at age's five to eight and ending at the ages of fourteen to eighteen.

Compulsory School Attendance Laws

State	Enactment[1]	Compulsory attendance, 2002
Alabama	1915	7–16
Alaska	1929	7–16
Arizona	1899	6–16[2]
Arkansas	1909	5–17[3]
California	1874	6–18
Colorado	1889	—
Connecticut	1872	7–18[4]
Delaware	1907	5–16[5]
District of Columbia	1864	5–18
Florida	1915	6–16[6]
Georgia	1916	6–16
Hawaii	1896	6–18
Idaho	1887	7–16
Illinois	1883	7–16
Indiana	1897	7–16
Iowa	1902	6–16[7]
Kansas	1874	7–18[4]
Kentucky	1896	6–16[8]
Louisiana	1910	7–17
Maine	1875	7–17
Maryland	1902	5–16
Massachusetts	1852	6–16
Michigan	1871	6–16
Minnesota	1885	7–16
Mississippi	1918	6–17
Missouri	1905	7–16
Montana	1883	7–16[9]
Nebraska	1887	7–16
Nevada	1873	7–17
New Hampshire	1871	6–16

New Jersey	1875	6–16
New Mexico	1891	5–18
New York	1874	6–16
North Carolina	1907	7–16
North Dakota	1883	7–16
Ohio	1877	6–18
Oklahoma	1907	5–18
Oregon	1889	7–18
Pennsylvania	1895	8–17
Rhode Island	1883	6–16
South Carolina	1915	5–16
South Dakota	1883	6–16
Tennessee	1905	6–17
Texas	1915	6–18
Utah	1890	6–18
Vermont	1867	6–16
Virginia	1908	5–18
Washington	1871	8–17[4]
West Virginia	1897	6–16
Wisconsin	1879	6–18
Wyoming	1876	6–16[2]

NOTE: (—) = not available.
1. Date of enactment of first compulsory attendance law.
2. Ages 6–16 or 10th grade completion.
3. Must have turned 17 by October 1.
4. Eligible for waiver.
5. Must have turned 5 by August 31.
6. Compulsory school age for all Manatee County Students who attained the age of 16 on or after October 1, 1999 is 18, unless the student has earned a high school diploma prior to reaching the 18th birthday.
7. Must have turned 16 by September 15.
8. Must have turned 6 by October 1.
9. Age 16 and completion of eighth grade.
Source: Department of Education, National Center for Educational Statistics, *Digest of Education Statistics, 2004.*Information Please® Database, © 2007 Pearson Education, Inc. All rights reserved.

The compulsory attendance act of 1852 enacted by the state of Massachusetts was the first general law attempting to control how children should be educated in the United States. The law included mandatory attendance for children between the ages of eight and fourteen for at least three month out of each year, of the twelve weeks at least six had to be consecutive. The exception to this attendance at a public school included: the child's attendance at another school for the same amount of time was proof that the child was taught the subjects, poverty, or the physical or mental ability of the child attend.

In 1873 the compulsory attendance was revised. The age limited was reduced to twelve but the annual attendance was increased to twenty weeks per year. Additionally truant officers were hired to check absences. By 1918, all states had passed a compulsory attendance law. Some of the current laws have been taken for early laws and have expanded on them, for example presently children are required to have a physical before entering school and again before enrolling in high school. They must also have a documentation of immunization shots in order to control disease in the schools. The compulsory attendance laws, for the most parts were adopted during the height of the industrial revolution in the nineteenth century. This was a time when the growth of industry opened new sources of income for families.

Early Years

The first public school in American was established by Puritan settlers in Boston in 1635. The public education in the United States developed from the roots in Puritan and Congregationalist religious schools in the 1600s. Subsequently the availability of free elementary education thanks to the efforts of Common School reform in the 1800s. The national system of formal education in the United State developed in the 19th century. Jefferson was the first American leader to suggest creating a public school system.

The most preliminary form of the public school was in the 1600s in the New England colonies of Massachusetts, Connecticut and New Hampshire. The primary belief on educating children was due to religious reasons. It was easy to implement, as the only group in existence were the Puritans and the Congregationalist. However, the influx of people from many countries and the fact that many had different faiths led to the weakening of the system. People refused to learn only in English and opposed clergy imposing their religious views through the public education. By the eighteenth century, private school had become the norm. After the Declaration of Independence, 14 states had their own constitutions and by 1791, out of the 14, 7 states had specific provision for education. Jefferson believed that education should be under the control of the government, free from religious biases and available to all people irrespective of their status in society.

The Beginning of the Public School System

Until the early 1840s, the education system was available to wealthy people. The Prominent Horace Mann from Massachusetts and Henry Barnard from Connecticut wanted all children to gain the benefits of an education. Mann stated the Common School Journal, which took the educational issues to the public. The common-school reformers argued for the case on the belief that common schooling could create good citizens unite society and prevent crime and poverty. As a result of their effort, free public education at the elementary level was available for all American children by the end of the 19th century. Massachusetts passed the first compulsory school attendance laws in 1852, followed by New York in 1853. By 1918 all states had passed laws requiring children to attend at least elementary. The Catholics were, however, opposed to common schooling and created their own private schools. Their decisions was supported by the 1925 Supreme Court rule in Pierce v. Society of Sisters, that states could not compel children to attend public schools, and that children could attend private schools. The first publicly supported secondary school in the United States was the Boston Latin School, founded in 1635. The attendance in secondary schools was very little because the curriculum was specialized and hard.

The demand for skilled workers in the middle eighteenth century led to Benjamin Franklin to start a new kind of secondary schools. As the 20th century progressed, most states enacted legislation extending compulsory education laws to the age of 16. It is essential to look at the history of the public education to be able to understand the laws that govern the systems as we know it today.

CHAPTER 2
Historical Facts about the America Education System

1635	The Boston Latin School, the first public funded secondary school in America, and the oldest educational institution in the country.
1779	Thomas Jefferson argued for universal taxpayer funded public education at the basic level, but was unsuccessful at this time.
1837	Horace Mann was the first secretary of education in the Commonwealth of Massachusetts.
1849	Henry Barnard creates a system of common schools in Connecticut.
1852	The Massachusetts legislature enacts the first compulsory education law requiring every child to get an education.
1853	New York follows the lead of Massachusetts and passes its own compulsory education law.
1865	By the end of the Civil War, most state constitution guaranteed public support for public education
1874	Michigan Supreme Court rules that communities could use property taxes to fund secondary schools.
1900	By this year 1.6 million children were attending public schools with 5% going on to high school.
1918	All states had compulsory education laws through elementary schools. John Dewey, an education professor at Columbia University Teacher's College advocates a theory of education called progressive education which eventually turned into the present day vocation education.
1920	High School becomes a more common experience.
1930	By this year, 29 million children attend public schools.
1950	By this year, 35% of public school students graduate from high school.
1954	The United States Supreme Court rules Brown v. Board of Education of Topeka that separate educational facilities for black and white children in the South are inherently unequal and unconstitutional.
1957	President Eisenhower orders federal troops to Little Rock, Arkansas to force racial integration of that city's Central High School. The Soviet Union launches Sputnik, the first spacecraft to orbit the earth, causing great concern in the United States about the state of science and math education in America.
1958	The National Defense Education Act passed by Congress in a reaction to the Russian launch of Spuntnik. The act provided federal funding to public schools to booster higher level science and math curriculum.
1965	Congress passes the Elementary and Secondary Education.
1968	Twelve cents of every dollar spent on K-12 education comes from the federal government.

1975	In the Education for all Handicapped Children Act, Congress orders the public schools to provide an education to all disabled children.
1979	President Jimmy Carter creates the new cabinet level Department of Education.
1983	A federal commission created by President Ronald Reagan publishes the report: A Nation at Risk.
2001	President George W. Bush reforms the Elementary and Secondary Education Act (ESEA) of 1965, to the No Child Left Behind Act.

Source: http://www.pbs.org/merrow/tv/trust/index.html
http://www.ed.gov

All children should be entitled to the same education service in the United States. For many years African- American communities has recognized and understood the important of education. More than fifty years ago African-American fought for the right to have the same educational opportunities as the Caucasian race. Since the victory of *Brown v. Broad of Education* some think that was the end of the struggle, however there is still a lot to be done to ensure that all children no matter; the color of their skin should be given the opportunity for educational excellence. This book is a guide to help parents understand that they have the right, the responsibility, to go to your child school and ask questions. Public schools are institutions that belong to all American citizens.

The education of African- American children is in a crisis. The public school systems that are operation today have left most African- American students behind. This is a problem for the nation not just the African-American communities. According to the National Education of Trust progress report card show that 61 percent of African- American 4th graders have not been taught a basic level in reading and 61 percent of African-American 8th graders do not meet the basic levels in math performance. According to the research data by the age of 17 African-American students math and reading skills will be the same as those of 13 year old Caucasians students. It is very clear that there is an achievement gap, researcher's data show that African-American student has been given fewer qualified teacher, weaker curriculum, and less money for their schools. As African- American parents must learn to fight for your child so they can get the education they deserve. In 2001 President George W. Bush reauthorized the federal law, Elementary and Secondary Education Act (ESEA) of 1965, which is now called the No Child Left behind Act (NCLB). The NCLB Act is a tool that parents can use to monitor their child school's performance. For parents to monitor their child's school performance one must first understand the No Child Left behind Act.

CHAPTER 3
Understand the NO Child Left Behind Act

What is the NO Child Left Behind Act?

According to the United State Department of Education: The No Child Left behind Act of 2001(NCLB) was signed into law on January 8th, 2002. This is a federal law that is built on four principles: accountability for results, more choices for parents, greater control and flexibility, and an emphasis on doing what work from scientific research.

What are the main sections of the No Child Left behind Act?

• Title I – Improving the Academic Achievement of the Disadvantaged
>	a. Improving Basic Programs Operated by Local Educational Agencies
>	b. Reading First

• Title II- Preparing, Training, and Recruiting High Quality Teachers and Principals
>	a. Teacher and Principal Training
>	b. Training, Recruiting, Teacher and Principal
>	C. Grant to States

• Title III- Language Instruction for Limited English Proficient and Immigrant Students

• Title IV- 21st Century Schools
>	a. Safe and Drug-Free Schools and Communities
>	b. 21st Century Community Learning Centers

• Title V-Promoting Informed Parents Choice and Innovative Programs
>	a. Innovative Programs

•Title VI -Flexibility and Accountability

• Title VII -Indian, Native Hawaiian and Alaska Native Education

• Title VIII-Impact Aid Program

•Title IX- General Provisions

•Title X- Repeals, Redefinitions and Amendments to other Statues

For the purpose of this guide Title I is the most important to be address. The purpose of Title I according to the United States Department of Education is to ensure that all children have a fair and equal opportunity to obtain a highly- quality education. The purpose can be accomplished according to the U.S Department of Education by:

(1). ensure high-quality academic assessment, accountability systems, and teacher preparation and training, curriculum, and instructional materials are aligned with State academic standards so that students, parents, teachers and administrators can measure progress against common expectation for student academic achievement.

(2). meet the educational needs of low-achieving children in the Nation's highest-poverty schools, limited English proficient children, migratory children, children with disabilities, Indian children, neglected or delinquent children and young children in need of reading.

(3) closing the achievement gap between high and low performing children especially the achievement gaps between minority and nonminority, disadvantage children and their advantage peers.

(4). hold schools, local educational agencies and States accountable for improving the academic achievement for all students,

(5) distributing and targeting resource sufficiently to make a difference to local education agencies and schools where the needs are the greatest.

(6). improving and strengthening accountability, teaching, and learning by using State assessment systems designed to ensure that students are meeting challenging State academic achievement and content standards and increasing achievement overall but especially for the disadvantaged.

(7) provide greater authority and flexibility to schools and teachers in exchange for greater responsibility for student performance

(8) provide children enriched and accelerated educational program, including the use of school wide programs or additional service that increase the amount and quality of instructional time.

(9) promoting school wide reform and ensuring the access of children to effective, scientifically based instructional strategies and challenging academic content.

(10) growth for professional development

(11) coordinate service under all parts of Title I

(12) given parents substantial and meaningful opportunities to participate in the education of their children.

Educational Agency GRANTS: For the purpose of carrying the NCLB according to the U.S. Department of Education

Fiscal Years	Amount
2002	$ 13,500,000,000
2003	$ 16,000,000,000
2004	$ 18,500,000,000
2005	$ 20,500,000,000
2006	$ 22,750,000,000
2007	$ 25,000,000,000

There are no questions that parents can be an important force in accelerating the school improvement of their child. The federal law No Child Left behind Act can help African-American parents to become an advocate, but this law can not stand along to improve the education of one child. For this law to serve the full potential to improving schools; parents and community groups must push to make sure that policies are implemented according to the intent of the law. The NCLB Act provides data that all parents especially African-American can use to evaluate the academic progress of their child school. Since, the passing of this law all public school systems are required to develop an effective process for encouraging parents involvement. The NCLB Act guarantees many right to all parents that include:

- Parents have the right to know your child's performance in mathematics, reading/language arts, and specific needs your child may have
- Parents have the right to know how your child's school is doing overall in comparison to the state academic standard and whether it is meeting annual state goals for student learning, called "Adequate Yearly Progress" or AYP.
- What is AYP? AYP is an individual's state's measure of progress toward the goal of 100 percent of students achieving to state academic standards in at least reading/language arts and math. Parents whose children are attending Title I (low-income) schools that do not make AYP over a period of years are given options to transfer their child to another school or obtain free tutoring(supplemental educational services).
- Parents have the right to be information about your child's school performance with groups of students, including African-American students. If any groups are not making AYP, the school must focus on making sure the students will.
- Parent have the right to know if your child is been taught by a teacher who is not fully qualified. Do not hesitate to ask your school principal about the qualifications of your child's teachers.
- What is the definition of a highly qualified teacher under the NCLB? To be highly qualified under the NCLB Act a teacher must: Have a bachelor's degree. Be fully certified as defined by the sate department of education; be able to demonstrate subject area competence in any core subject (Mathematics, English, Social Studies and Science).
- NCLB Act provides funds for some students to be transfer to higher-performing schools or get tutoring to raise their academic achievement. Parents should ask their child's school principal whether NCLB Act gives their child the right to be transfer or receives after school tutoring. Parents do no have to pay for this service-the school district

receives federal funds for this purpose. Each local educational agency that applies for assistance shall describe how it will provide the low-achieving schools the necessary resource to meet goals according to the NCLB Act.

•Remember when parents are involved in their child education child do better in school. The NCLB Act has provided some leverage for parents and advocates to help with understand how to help with the improvement of their child education.

Understanding the NCLB Act is only part of the picture, how well students are learning is another part. Parents need to know whether their children are getting the help and support from their school. Parents should not be intimidated by the school data; one does not have to be a statistician to understand your child's school data. Schools have the responsibility to educate all children to high standards; the NCLB Act is federal a law that provides parents with the opportunity to see that school systems are reformed to meet the need of all students.

Parents have the power to see that their children receive an education with high standard; it the responsibility of all students, parents, teachers, and communities to work together to foster an environment where students can learn. In today society, a high school diploma is no longer enough. In sprite of the belief that public schools should be available to every child irrespective of race, gender or economic status, this has not happened in reality. The American public school is a system that looks upon as a system that inculcates the ideas of equality and education for all. The pitfall of the public school system has cause many African-American students to be left behind. The NCLB Act is a plan by the government to ensure that all students have an opportunity to receive a good education. Since the 1950's, public policy toward education has addressed issues in education, the federal government has especially been concerned with issues of equality in all schools districts.

The reauthorized of ESEA (1965), is very clear about what students need to know and should be able to do. Today the ESEA (1965) which is the NCLB Act is base on four basic principles: *stronger accountability for parent and teachers, increasing flexibility and local control, expand option for parents, and emphasis on effective teaching methods. Basically, the law mandates state administered standardized testing, flexibility with school budget (allocation of funds various (NCLB programs), parental option in regards to sending their child to better school than their home school, and innovative professional development in reading programs.* In an article written by Northwest Evaluation Association title, Achievement Gaps: AN EXAMINATION of DIFFERENCES in STUDENT ACHEIEVMENT AND GROWTH, the study shows that at the end of each grade European-American students perform better than African-American and Hispanic students. In general this study as well as other studies show that students enrolled in high poverty schools begin schools with lower skills this phenomenon is observed at each grade level in the public school system. Minority children are less likely to be recommended or enrolled in challenging courses in elementary, middle or high school. The purpose of this guide is to give parents a tool to ensure that at an early age their children are given the opportunities to the best education possible. The foundation of the family is the key to improving the education of all children.

CHAPTER 4
What Parents Need To Know About?
Assessments/IEP/504 Plans

In the current debate about nation wide educational restricting, perhaps no issue is more central to the concerns of equity than that of student assessment. Awareness of how standardized testing shapes curriculum and teaching highlights the links between assessment and educational equality. Yet, there is no consensus about the role of student assessment or educational reform. A few educators believe that excellence and equality, in education can be achieved by identifying student's strengths as well as their needs and to determine the most appropriate and effective means of assessing their ability through assessments. The pressure of assessments has exploded. Across the board, school jurisdictions are developing and utilizing all types of assessments.

The Annual Yearly Progress (AYP) requirements of No Child Left Behind Act underscore both the mandate and the challenge of assuring that student with Individualize Education Programs (IEP), 504 Plans and English Language Learner (ELL) achieve the same high standards of performance that are expected of their peers. The indeed is laudable; states, districts, schools and teachers must be accountable for the learning of students with special needs as are the students themselves. These subgroups can no longer be invisible in the educational system; their learning needs must be met, and they too must make steady progress. According to the NCLB Act all students must be judged proficient on statewide testing by the year of 2014 (Lecker, 2005). Already, the NCLB Act results suggest a different reality: African-American, Hispanic and special needs subgroups are being left behind and schools districts serving significant proportions of these students are less likely to meet the AYP goals and more likely to be subject to corrective action. There are many reasons why students with special needs lag behind. Research shows that economically disadvantaged and culturally diverse subgroups have had less access than other students to a challenging curriculum that would prepare then for success by today's standards (Gulton & Oakes, 1995).

Under the NCLB Acts students in the public schools systems throughout the country must participate in annual testing in specific academic area. The NCLB Acts does not address the issues of whether or not a student must pass a test in order to move on to the next grade or to graduate. This decision is made by each state department of education. The focus of the NCLB Acts is on ensuring that school makes AYP as reflected in annual tests. States are required to have annual assessment in reading, math grades 3rd and 8th, once between 10-12 graders. States are required to assess all children in science at least once between the grader 3rd through 5th grade; 6th through 9th and 10th through 12th.

Fairness demands that all students have equitable opportunity to learn especially if assessments carry significant future consequences. Moreover, if NCLB Acts goals are to be met and the achievement gap reduced, schools must move beyond the performance orientation by the AYP and to understand why results are as they are and how to improve them. The opportunity for students with special needs is unlikely to improve until students have more effective's opportunities to attain expected standards. In order to judge if students are being given the optimum chance to meet expected standards, the following questions must be asked: are students being given opportunities? What do effective opportunities look like?

According to the article: Assessment: A Key Component of Education Reform by Dr. Martha L. Turlow, assessment is a key component of special education and education reform. She also stated that children are assessed individually to determine their eligibility for special education services and to ascertain learning needs. Assessments are designed to measure the status of the education system for all students. (Thurlow, p.1).

Today's assessments are a combination of selected response (multiples choices), brief constructed responses and extended responses. These formats are different from those of the past such as true/false, matching and filling in the blanks. However, alternative assessments are being used in various districts and through out the state. Some alternative assessments may include: problem solving, experiments, plays, hand-on activities, and journals, portfolios of student work, computer simulations and self assessments (Thurlow, p.1).

The United states Department of Education says that the NCLB Act is designed to change the culture of America's Schools by closing the achievement gap, offering more flexibility, giving parents more options, and teaching students based on what works. Under the act's accountability provisions, states must describe how they will close the achievement gap and make sure all students, including those who are disadvantaged, achieve academic proficiency. They must produce annual state and school district report cards that inform parents and communities about state and school progress. Schools that do not make progress must provide supplement services, such as free tutoring or after-school assistance; take corrective actions; and, if still not making adequate yearly progress after five years, make dramatic changes to the way the schools are run (Paige Approve Maryland State Accountability, April 1, 2003).Children's academic performance; behavior and social skills are good when parents are involved. Here are some ways that you as parents can actively participate in your child's education.

1. Make sure that you know the State Department of Education Website
2. Make sure that you know the Local Department of Education Website
3. Know the teacher names and subject taught.
4. Visit the assessments links on the state website.
5. Know the date and time of all state assessments.
6. On going communication between teachers and parent is important, whether via phone, e-mail, or school-based meeting.
7. Always attendance Back-to-School night, since teachers are the best source to learn more about your child's academic performance and how to prepare for the school year.
8. Keep a log of your child's report cards, all state test result, and progress report.
9. Know your child's reading level; for example your child could be in the ninth grade but could be reading on a fifth grade level.
10. Know your child's math level; for example your child could be in the ninth grade but have not master the basic skill from grade 1-8.
11. Organization skills is a must, teach your child how to organize his or her materials by subjects and most of all always talk to your child everyday about school. Communicate is the key.

12. Make sure that when you seek help from education services for tutoring that the company understands the state assessment. Most of the time tutoring service works on skills that your child is having problems with and the programs are not the same as the school curriculum.

Facts you may uncover may be difficult, even painful, for you to hear. The work to improve students performance in school might not be easy, but until issues are fully confronts the school communities cannot move and improve your child performance in schools. The Parents the Family Educational Right and Privacy (FERPA) is a federal law that gives you the right to have access to your child's education records, the right to seek to have the records amended, and the right to have some controls over the disclosure of personal identifiable information from the education records. Always take the time to review the information in your child's record. When a student turnn18 years of age or enter a postsecondary institutions at any age, the rights of the FERPA is transfer from the parents to the student.

Individualized Education Plan and 504 Plans

According to the National Education Association (NEA), access to free, quality education is the key to the American promise of equal opportunity. This promise was formally extended to children with disabilities with the passing in 1975 of landmark federal legislation now known as the Individuals with Disabilities Act (IDEA). Public schools now serve numerous children with a wide array of disabling conditions (NEA: Special Education-IDEA, p.1).

The NEA also reports that special education issues affect general programs in a number of ways. Over the years, the number of United States students enrolled in special education programs have increased. This research also indicates that three out of every four students with disabilities spend parts or all of their time in a general classroom. In turn, nearly every general education classroom in this country includes students with disabilities. Each school and school district must develop the best way to conduct programs and figure out how to pay for them (NEA-Special Education-IDEA, p.2). For parents to understand Individualized Education Plan (IEP) and 504 Plans one must first understand the following terms:

Definitions

The following two terms were defined by the website: www.weac.org- (special education inclusion):

⊠ **Inclusion**: is a term which expresses commitment to educate each child, to the maximum extent appropriate, in the school and classroom he or she would otherwise attend. It means bringing the support services to the child.

⊠ **Full Inclusion:** means that all students, regardless of handicapping conditions or severity will be in regular classroom/program full time. All services must be given to the child in that setting.

The following terms are defined according to Bateman & Bateman 2001:

☒ **Individualized Education Program (IEP):** The IEP is a contract between the districts and the student's parents or guardians. The IEP formalizes specifics goals and objectives for the student.

☒ **Individuals with Disabilities Education Act**: (formerly known as Public Law 105- 17 mandates that all children with disabilities between the ages of 3 and 21, regardless of the types of severity of their disabilities, will receive a free, appropriate public education in the least restrictive environment.

☒ **504 plan**: To be eligible under §504, a student must be "qualified" and "handicapped." "Handicapped" (a term which has been replaced with "disabled") is defined as follows. any person who: has a physical or mental impairment which **substantially limits** one or more major life activities (such as: caring for one's self, performing manual tasks, walking, seeing, hearing, speaking, breathing, learning, working), has a record of such impairment, or is regarded as having such an impairment.

504 Plans vs. IEP

504	IEP
• Accommodations	• Accommodations
	• Times lines
	• Assessments
	• Goals and Objectives
	• Least Restrictive Environment
	• Eligibility
	• Program
	• Complaints and Disagreements

Individuals with Disabilities Education Act (IDEA) has many more restricting for qualifications, but also provides more specialized services and safeguards. Under IDEA and IEP is created for each child who qualifies. The passing of the IDEA have giving parents with special needs an opportunity to be a crucial member of their child's education team. Parents can now work closely with educators to help develop the IEP for their child. The IEP describes goals the team's sets for a child during the school year, as well as any special support needed to help the child achieve.

Who Needs an IEP?

A child who has difficulty learning, functioning, and struggling in school might be identified and quality or be a perfect candidate for an IEP. The student may qualify for support service which allows the student to be taught in a special way, for reasons such as: learning disabilities, attention deficit hyperactivity disorder (ADHD), emotional disorders, autism, hearing impairment, visual impairment, speech or language impairment and development delay. The goal of IDEA is to ensure that each child is educated in the least restrictive environment possible, effort is always made to help the child stay in a regular classroom. However, child might be place in a special class. These classes have fewer students per teacher, which allow the teacher to give more individualized attention to the student. Usually the teacher has specific training in help student with special education needs.

Referral and Evaluating Process

The referral process generally begins with a teacher, parent, or a doctor who identifies or have concerned that a child might be having trouble in school. Teachers are usually the first to identify a problem. Usually a teacher will notify the school counselor or the school psychologist when they identify a student struggling with their academic. The first step of the process is to notify the parents. The second step should be to gather specific data regarding the student's progress and this can be done by: a conference with the parents, student, observation of the student and most of all a analysis of the student's performance (attention, behavior, completing task in class, tests score, class work and homework). This information helps school personnel determine specific strategies that can be implemented to help the child be successful in school. If the specific strategies don't work, the child could be tested for a specific learning disability. It's important to note, that the presence of a disability don't automatically guarantee a child will receive services. To be eligible, the disability must affect the child's functioning at school. To determine eligibility a team or professionals will evaluate the child based on the observations; the child performance on standardized tests, daily work on test, class work, homework, and behavior. The professional team could include:

- ⊠Psychologist

- Speech Therapist

- Physical Therapist

- Special Educator

- Occupational Therapist

- Vision or Hearing Specialist

- Others, depending on the child's specific needs.

As parents, you have the right to decide whether to have your child assessed. If you choose you will be asked to sign permission form that will detail who is involved in the process and the types of tests that will be used. The tests might include measure of a specific skills such as reading, math, development skills such as speech and language. Testing does not necessarily mean that your child will receive service. Once the testing is completed a comprehensive evaluation report is done to comply the finding. The parents then are given a chance to review the report before an IEP is developed. Some parent will disagree with the report, but parents have the opportunity and the right to work together with the school to come up with a plan that best meets the child's needs.

Developing an IEP

An IEP is an educational plan developed for your child. If a child receives special education services, the IDEA requires that the child have an IEP. If you are parents that receive a letter or a phone call inviting you to an IEP meeting, most of the time it is with anxiety. As parents one might be confused or asked your self these questions: What is my role, what should I do or not do. As the parents you have a unique role to play in the IEP process. As the parent, you are a member of the IEP team. Before the IEP Team can develop an appropriate plan (IEP) for your child, the child's problem must be accurately identified and described. To make an accurate diagnosis, the IEP team needed together information from many sources. This information should include the observations of the child in various environments, which should include home and school. The IEP should accurately describe your child's learning problems and how the problem is going to be dealt with. Program placement should depend on: Least restrictive Environment. This means the students are not to be segregated from the general education setting unless absolutely necessary.

The IEP document should contain a statement of the child's present levels of educational performance. Education decision-making is similar to medical decision-making. When medical specialists confront a problem, they gather information from diagnostic test they provide them with objective information. Educational decision-making includes observation by people who know the child well and objective information from various test and assessments. The IEP is similar to a medical treatment plan the principles are the same. The IEP should include: information about the child's present levels of performance in reading and math, goal and objectives for the child, measurable annual goals, short and long terms goals, the goals should be related to the child's needs and disability and most of all the goals and objectives should meet the educational needs that result for your child disability. The IEP development process should involve main points which are:

- ⊠ meeting with you, your child, school staff member, place and time
  Parents and the school agree on when and where the meeting should take place.
  The meeting can happen before, during or after school
  By law the school must tell you in writing: purpose, time, place who will be there and
  That you can invite other people who are knowledge of your child disability

- written document
The IEP must be done 30 calendar days from the date your child become eligible
You must agree to the IEP, in writing before the school can care out the IEP
The IEP must be reviewed at least once every 12 month this is called the annual review

- ⊠It may take more than one meeting to write the IEP, if you feel more time is needed
  Ask the team to schedule another meeting, you can ask for an IEP meeting at any time
  The best time to asked for an IEP to make changes, if you needed to is at the end of a grading period.

Who attend the IEP Meeting?

Under IDEA, certain people must be part of the IEP Team. The Team is made of the following persons:

●☒ Parent(s) or Guardian: As a parent you know your child better than anyone. You know the child's strengths and weakness, you can give insight to what your child like or dislikes. Your job at the IEP meeting is to: learn and understand the process, share information, asked questions, offer suggestion that will work for your child, and keep the team focus on the needs of your child.

●☒ School Administrator: a member of the school staff who oversees the meeting. This person must understand the school curriculum and should also be qualified to provide special education services. The administrator at the IEP meeting must know what resources the school has available.

●☒Special Education Teacher: at least one of your child special education teachers. The special educator usually has been involved in your child evaluation, understand the result and can explain and interpret the results to the team. Usually the educator can explain different teaching styles and instructional methods that can be used to help meet your child's needs. The special educator can talk about lessons that may need to be adapted or modified to help your child learn. In many schools, the special educators are to make sure that all involved follow the IEP as written.

●☒General Education Teacher: at least one of your child general education teachers. The general education teacher knows the curriculum for your child's grade level. In the general education classroom the general educator's teacher will talk about what your child will be taught and expect to learn. The support and service might include adapting the curriculum, providing lower reading levels materials, using graphic organizer, and how the child will be helped to make sure that the goals listed in the IEP is done.

●☒Evaluation Personnel: someone who knows about your child evaluation, evaluation results what the result means in turn of instruction.

●☒Child: If the team will be taking about transition after high school your child must be invited to the meeting, otherwise when and how your child participates in the IEP meeting is a decision of you and your child.

Beside the people listed above, you and the school can invite other to the IEP meeting than can include:

●☒ Therapist: a person who is knowledgeable of your child

● Interpreters: if English is not your first language or if you communicate by using sign the law says that an interpreter must be provide for if you ask

• Advocate: a person with knowledge of your child such as a tutor, educational consultants, or staff members at the school, friend, both you and the school have the right to invite other individuals to join the team.

IEP DOCUMENT

In each state or school district the IEP can look different but under the IDEA, the items below must be in every IEP

• Child's present levels of educational performance:
This section of the IEP describes how your child is doing in school. The information is based on current information usually no more than one year. The present levels of performance should cover all area of development where the child might need support. Examples are: Academic skills: math reading, writing

- ☒Social Skills: making friends

- ☒ Behavior

- ☒Communication skills: talking

- ☒ Mobility: school/ and the community

- ☒ Vocational skills working

At the present level information about your child's disability affects his or her involvement in the general curriculum; in other words, you and the team talks about the impact of your child's disability. Information that you, teachers and others share can be included in your child's present level. A well written present level will describe:

- ☒ your child's strengths and weakness

- ☒ what strategies that will help your child learn

- ☒ what limits or interferes with your child's learning

- ☒ how the child's disability affects their ability to be in general education classes

Below are examples of a well-written IEP for a 4th grader with learning disabilities:

Example 1

The result of standardized testing using the Woodcock-Johnson (W-J-R) show your(*child name)* reading skills are at a 3rd grade level(standard score = 89). His or Her basic writing skills are at 3.7 grade level (standard score = 81). {Objective date of the evaluation}.

His or Her performance in basic reading and writing is significantly below his or her ability. (*Child name*) makes errors when he or she reads and have difficulty decoding long words {weakness}, but his or her comprehension skills are strong {strength}. (Child name) uses context reading {what helps learning}. He or she has a strong reading vocabulary {strength}.

When writing, (*Child name*) frequently misspells words and uses incorrect punctuation {weakness}. It is much easier for (child name) to express himself or herself by speaking rather than by writing. He or she sometimes gets frustrated when writing and hurries through written work {what hinders learning}

Example 2

(*Child name*) is essentially non-verbal and uses many ways to communicate including: gestures, facial expression, eye gaze, vocalization, word approximations, head nod for yes; He or she needs a quiet, separate place to do individual work. He or she learns quickly when working in a small group. He or she understands and remembers what he or she hears about a subject. Learning by reading or looking at pictures is difficult and doesn't work as well for him.

• Annual Goals and Short-term Objectives

Once your child's needs are identified, the IEP team works to develop appropriate goals and objectives to address your child's disability. *Annual Goals* describes what your child can expect to do within a 12 month period. A *short-term* objective is steps that will help your child reach the annual goal. The goals and objectives should be written. Writing goals and objectives can be one of the hardest parts of the IEP. One reason is goals and objective can cover so many different areas. Depending upon your child's needs, some goals and objective may target area of the general curriculum. A well-written goal should be (a) positive and (b) describe a skill that can be seen and measured. It answers the questions:

• Who?… will achieve?

  • What?……skill or behavior?

  • How?…… in what manner or at what level?

  • Where?….. in what setting or under what conditions?

  • When?….by what time? Or ending date?

Example of an Annual Goal and Short-term Objectives:

{*Child Name*} will achieve a reading score at the 4th grade level as measure by the Qualitative Reading Inventory (QRI)

Short –term Objective:

1. Given a list of 10 unfamiliar words that contain short-vowel sounds, (*child name*) will decode them with 80% accuracy on each of 6 trials.

2. Given a list of 10 unfamiliar words that contain long-vowel sounds, (*child name*) will decode them with 80% accuracy on each of the 6 trials.

3. {*Child Name*} will correctly pronounce 20 words with 80% accuracy on each of the 6 trials to demonstrate understanding of the rule that where one vowel follows another, the first vowel is pronounced with a long sound and the second vowel is silent.

4. {*Child Name*} will correctly separate 20 words by syllables with 80% accuracy on each of the 6 trials to demonstrate understanding of the rule that each syllable in a word must contain a vowel.

5. {*Child Name*} will demonstrate understanding of the meaning of new words by answering comprehension questions on weekly teacher-made vocabulary test with 80% accuracy.

Measuring Your Child's Progress

Effective's goals and objectives are critical parts of your child's IEP. Keeping track of your child's progress is very important. How will you and the school work together as a team to make sure that your child reaches the goals by the end of the school year. This information must be included in the IEP. The IEP team must *decide: how your child's progress will be measured, when your child's progress will be measured, how well your child needs to perform in order to achieve the objective, and how you will be regularly informed of your child's* progress. Information on how well your child must perform and how his or her progress will be measured is included in the short-term objective this type of information is called the *evaluation criteria*. This tells how the student will be evaluated.

Well-written *evaluation criteria* are stated in objective, measureable terms. Often, this progress is measured by numbers or scores as shown in the examples above. Other way the IEP team could stated the objective are: Give a list of 10 unfamiliar words that contain short-vowel sounds, {*child name*} will decode them with: *60% accuracy by December 4, 75% accuracy by March 5, 90% accuracy by June 20*. In other instances, progress is not measured in number scores: By June 20, (*child name*) will complete the course tasks adapted by the teacher. In this case the teacher will observe and check the student progress. Other ways of checking the student progress may include: reviewing class work, homework assignments; giving quizzes, tests, or teacher-made assessments and formal and informal assessments.

A List of Typical Special Education Accommodations

Individualized accommodations are puts into place to help learners at risk and students with special needs to have success in school. This is a typically list of, accommodations that are sometime in students IEP for a variety of disabilities.

●{ Graphic Organizers

●{ Provide photo copied of notes to avoid having these students copying from the board or overhead.

●{ Give ongoing feedback

●{ Seat the child away from distractions whenever possible Think critically about seating arrangements.

●{ Provide time extensions as necessary

●{ Make sure the teacher gives repetition and clarification regularly

●{ Color code items

●{ Provide extra time for the procession of information

●{ Provide organization tips and lets parents know about the organization tips they can be use to support the student at home.

●{ Progress Sheet: provide a progress sheet of expected assignments for the day/week

●{ Make sure there are visual clues around the classroom

●{ Provide time management skills

●{ Large size print

●{ Use of technology when necessary

●{ Keep lesson concrete, use visual aids and keep the materials concrete

●{ Provide close proximity to the teacher

●{ Let the child provide oral responses instead of written where appropriate to demonstrate understanding of concepts.

●{ Provide auditory supports to avoid the student having too much text to read.

504 of the Rehabilitation Act of 1973

According to this law, parents of qualifying children have the right to develop a Section 504 plan with their child's school. To qualify for protection under Section 504, a child must have a record of such impairment, or be regarded as having such impairment. Schools can lose federal funding if they do not comply with the law. Section 504 of the Rehabilitation Act of 1973 guarantees an appropriate special education as well as accessibility to regular education programs. It requires that all children with disabilities be provided a free, appropriate pubic education in the least restrictive environment. A person with a disability under Section504 is any person who (i) has a physical or mental impairment which substantially limits one or more major life activities, (ii) has a record of such impairment, or (iii) is regarded as having such impairment. This definition differs from that found in the (IDEA), which defines specific disabling conditions. Because of this difference, some individuals who are not qualified for special education under IDEA may be qualified for special services under the 504. In addition to students who are eligible under the definition of Section 504 but not under definition of IDEA, there may also be students who have a disability according to both definitions but do not require special education. For example, some students who use wheelchairs may qualify under both definitions. The student might not require special education service in the classroom, but they might require special accommodations under Section 504. IDEA has many more restrictions for qualifications, but also provides more specialized services and safeguards.

Discipline Student with Disabilities

The IDEA (2004) contains important changes to the ways schools can discipline students with disabilities. Since students with specific learning disabilities (SLD) make up roughly half of the students receiving special education services, understanding these changes is an important part of being your child advocate. According to the United State Department of Education, Office of Special Education, and Rehabilitative Services, Office of Special Education Programs, 26th Annual Report to Congress on the implementation of the IDEA, Washington, D.C. 2006, in the school year of 2001-2002 students with specific learning disabilities represented:

- 52 percent of all special education students who were suspended for 10 schools days or less

- 48 percent of all special education students who were suspended for more than 10 school days or expelled

- 60 percent of all special education students who were removed from their School Placement due to possession of drugs or weapons.

Like all students, those with disabilities can be suspended or expelled for violating the school's rule and school code of conduct. However, IDEA provides specifics procedures that school must follow when discipline a student with disabilities. These procedures were put into IDEA (2004) to prevent schools from suspending or expelling students without considering the effects of the child's disability. IDEA 2004 provides schools with the authority to consider and unique circumstances on a case-by-case basis when making a determination to discipline a student with a disability. Schools have the responsibility to make sure that all students understand the school's code of conduct. Your child's IEP team should determine any specialized instruction in the IEP that will address your child's behavior. A behavior intervention plan can be use to help with appropriate classroom behavior. IDEA (2004) provides flexibility for school personnel who are often operating within a district's *zero-tolerance policy. A zero-tolerance policy* usually requires school personnel to follow a suspension or expulsion policy of any student who violates the school code of conduct regardless of the circumstances. In all cases, the disciplinary action considered for students with disabilities must be the same for all students, in other words, school personnel may not increase a student's suspension because of the student's disability.

Whenever school personnel decide to discipline a student with a disability by removing the student from the current educational setting, the school must notify the parents on the same day the decision is made and provide the parents with a written copy of the school *Procedure Safeguards Notice.*

IDEA 2004 Discipline Rules:

For disciplinary actions lasting 10 school days or less

●{ A student with a disability who has an IEP in effect can be disciplined like any other student who violates the school code of conduct.

●{ Parents can request that the school continue educational services for the student during the time of the disciplinary action or allow the parents to facilitate the student's completion of the school work, while the school is not required to grant such requests, many will agree so that the student doesn't fall behind.

For disciplinary actions resulting in removal of more than 10 schools days in the same year (whether or not the days are consecutive):

●{ The school must provide special education services that allow the student to: continue to participate in the general education curriculum although in another setting, and progress toward meeting the goals outlined in the student's IEP.

●{ If the action *does not result in exclusion* from school for more than 10 consecutive schools day and does not constitute a change of placement, school personnel must determine what services the student should be provided. (Note: a change or placement occurs when the student is excluded from his/her current placement for more than 10 consecutive school days in a school year or upon the 11th school day that a child is excluded from his/her current placement when there is evidence of a pattern of a series of removals).

●{ If the disciplinary actions *results in an exclusion* from school that is a change of placement, the student IEP team must meet to determine the exact educational services needed while the student is assigned to the alternative educational setting.

●{ Within the 10 days from the beginning of a disciplinary *action that results in an exclusion that exceeds 10 school days* the school district, the parents, and members of the students IEP team must meet to determine if the conduct in question was caused by, or had a direct and substantial relationship to the student's disability. The team must also determine if the conduct was the direct result of the school's failure to implement the student's IEP, including a behavioral intervention plan. If the group decides that the student's behavior was a direct result of the school's failure to implement the deficiencies and return the student to his/her original placement.

Manifestation Determination-How is Behavioral Related to Disability

IDEA 2004 has made some significant changes to the manner in which a determination is made about the relationship between the student's behavior that lead to the disciplinary action, and the student disability. In making the manifestation determination, the IEP team must: review the student's IEP, the student's behavior intervention plan, teacher observation and relevant information provided by the parents. Under IDEA 2004 the presumption of a connection between behavior and disability no longer exists, now the team is required to answer these questions:

1. Considering the behavior subject to discipline, review the student's behavior to determine if it was caused by, or had a direct and substantial relationship to the student's disability. For example, a student's low-esteem, while possibly a by-product of a learning disability, is not alone sufficient to be considered a basis for finding a direct relationship between the student's disability and behavior.

2. Did the school fail to follow a portion of the IEP including a behavior intervention plan in a manner that directly caused the misconduct?

3. If the behavior is found to be directly related to the student's disability, the IEP team must plan for a functional behavioral assessment and the development of a behavioral intervention plan based on the results of that assessment. If the student already had a behavior intervention plan in place, the IEP team must review if the plan was being followed and revise it as needed to address the problem behavior that led to the disciplinary action.

4. For students whose behavior was not directly related to the disability, the same disciplinary actions can be imposed as those imposed on a non-disabled student. Such action could include expulsion. However, if student is expelled from school, the student must continue to receive educational services that allows him or her to continue to participate in the general education curriculum and progress toward meeting the goals set in the IEP.

5. Be on the alert for the Special Circumstance, certain offense can lead to a student being moved to an alternative educational setting for up to 45 school days even if the conduct is determined to be related to the student's disability. Removing a student for these offense lists below does not require parent permission or agreement, nor does it require any involvement by a hearing. These offenses are: *Weapons: if a student carrier or possesses a weapon, on the way to or at school, on school premise, at a school function. Drugs: if a student knowingly possesses or uses illegal drugs or sells or solicits the sale of illegal drugs while at school or at a school function. Serious bodily injury: if a student inflicted serious bodily injury upon another person, while at*

school, on school premise or at a function at schools.

6. Additional provision allows a school to seek to remove a student for up to 45 school days if the school believes that returning the student to the same educational setting is substantially likely to result in injury to the student or other students. The school must do this by making a request to a hearing officer, who, among other requirements, it not employed by the state education agency or local school district involved in educating the child; has specialized knowledge and skills related to IDEA and has no interest that conflict with his objectively in the hearing process.

Parent Right to Appeal

Parent has the right to challenge any decision made regarding the alternative educational setting or the determination regarding the *manifestation determination* by asking for a due *process hearing*. School can also request for due *process hearing* if school personnel feel that returning a student to school is highly likely to result in injury to student or other students. In either case, the hearing must be expedited by: holding the hearing 20 school days of the date of the requested, and issue a decision by the hearing officer within 10 school days after the hearing. IDEA 2004 made an important change to the placement of student during the appeal process. Before, a student was to remain in his or her current educational placement during the appeal process-often referred to as stay put. Now, under IDEA 2004, the student remains in the alternative educational setting, unless the parent and the state agree otherwise or to the period for the infraction has expired.

Under certain circumstances, the protections available to a student with a disability who is already eligible for special education services may also be available to a student who does not have in IEP an effect. These circumstances may apply to student:

- •{ if the child's parent has expressed concern in writing to the school personnel, including the teacher that their child may be in need of special education prior to the behavior that resulted in the disciplinary action.

- •{ If the child's parent had requested an evaluation, preferably in writing, as Provided for by IDEA

- •{ If child's teacher or other school personnel expressed concerns about a pattern ob behavior that might call for a referral for evaluation, such concerns would need to have been made directly to supervisory personnel at the school building or school district level. For example, a teacher expressing his or her concerns to a parent would not be considered an adequate basis of knowledge. Certain exceptions apply to the above circumstances they included: if the child parent had not allowed an evaluation of the child or had refused education service that had been as required by IDEA; if the child has been evaluated as

27

required by IDEA and was not found eligible for special education services. IDEA's regarding the discipline of student with disabilities are complex and often confusing, but IDEA focuses on improve the lives of learning students with learning disabilities.

Five keys points that parents should remember about IEP:

1.An IEP is a written document that's developed for an individual child who's eligible for special education services.

2.Parents must be invited and are expected to be fully participants in the meeting.

3.The IEP is a document written by public schools for students who qualify for special education. It applies whether they attend public schools or have been placed by the public school in a private school setting.

4.The IEP must be reviewed at least annually during the school year. However, it may be reviewed more frequently if requested by a parent or teacher because or lack of academic progress.

5.An IEP must be developed to meet the unique needs of a child with a disability who requires special education services to benefit from general education program.

Appropriate Assessment Accommodations for Students with Disabilities

Under the NCLB Act public school students must participate in annual testing in specific academic areas and grades outline in the law, including students with disabilities. According to the NCLB Act, students with disabilities, and those cover under of IDEA or Section 504 of the Rehabilitation Act must be provided with appropriate accommodations necessary to participate in state assessments because schools are held accountable for the achievement of all students.

Accommodations are tools and procedure that provide equal access to instruction assessment for students with disabilities. Accommodations are not the same as modification. Policies regarding standard and non-standard testing accommodations differ by state. All IEP/504 team members need to be familiar with state policies and guideline regarding the use of assessment accommodations. All members should know: the test content, types of questions, and testing conditions, the test guideline, and what accommodations will invalidate a test score. All students with IEP and 504 plans are entitled to the appropriate accommodations that allow students to fully participate in state-and district wide testing. The student's IEP /504 teams select the accommodations for both instruction test and state assessments. Once the accommodations have been selected the use of the accommodations should be consistently. Each teacher must be informed of the accommodations. Each teacher of the student must implement the accommodations when testing the student in the classroom.

Presentation Accommodations: Student with print disabilities defined as difficulty or inability to visually read standard print because of physical sensory or cognitive disability

Questions: Can the student read and understand direction?
Does the student need direction repeated?
Has the student been identified as having a reading Disability?

Accommodations: Large print ; Human reader; Talking materials (calculators, clocks, timers)

Source: National Center for Learning Disabilities

Setting Accommodations: Student, who that easily distracted in large group setting, concentrates best in small groups.

Questions: Do others easily distract the students?
Does student have trouble staying on task?
Does student exhibit behaviors that would disrupt other students?

Accommodations: Change of room or locations

Source: National Center for Learning Disabilities

Response accommodations: Student with physical, sensory or learning disabilities(including difficulties with memory sequencing, directionally, alignment and organization)

Questions: Can the student use a pencil or other writing instrument?
Does the student have a disability that affects his or her ability to spell?
Does the student have trouble with tracking from one page to another and Maintaining her/his place?

Accommodations: Note-takers, tape recorder, spelling and grammar device, graphic Organizers,

Source: National Center for Learning Disabilities

Timing & Scheduling Accommodations: Students who need more time, cannot concentrate for extended periods, have health-related disabilities, special/or medications needs.

Questions: Can student work continuously during the entire time allocated for test Administration?
  Does student tire easily because of health?
  Does student need shorter working periods and frequent breaks?

Accommodations: Extended time, Frequent Breaks, Multiple test session

Source: National Center for Learning Disabilities

It is imperative for parents to understand the requirement of their child accommodations

CHAPTER 5
A Parent's Guide To Kindergation To Fifth Grade

Curriculum

The public school kindergarten and elementary school curriculum varies in states. The kindergarten curriculum focuses on the foundational skills necessary for early reading and writing success. The goal of any school systems is to provide programs for all students to achieve proficiency at all grade levels. This chapter will provide an overview of what students should know and be able to do at grade levels by subjects. Information in the tables in this chapter is a guide to give parents the opportunity to have ideas and be knowledgeable of what their child is expected to know from kindergarten to fifth grade.

Kindergarten

Reading
• **Oral Language:** Participants in speaking recite short poems, rhymes and songs Use number words, use words to describe actions, people, and things, Ask why and how questions, follow rules for conversations and expands word choices to communicate effectively.   • **Reading**: Understand how print is organized and read left to right, front to back, and top to bottom, identify, read and explain own writing and drawing, identify common signs and logos.   • **Phonemic Awareness**: Identifies and generate rhyming words, identifies words beginning with the same sounds, blends sounds together to make words.   • **Phonics**: Recognizes and identifies all upper and lower case letters, match consonant sounds to appropriate letters.   • **Comprehensions**: Learns concepts about print by tracks words from left to right, top to bottom, identifies parts of a book; learn reading strategies used before, during and after reading.   • **Before Reading Strategies**: determine a purpose for reading, use background knowledge and preview text to make predictions and ask questions.   • **During-Reading Strategies**: Understand characters, setting, problem/solving and plot when reading for a literary experiences; drawing to identifies cause/effect and conclusions   • **After-Reading**: Responds to reading through discussion, summarizes text and responds to comprehension questions in writing.   • **Writing:** Print own names, draw a picture to communicate, begin using letter to spell the sounds they hear.

Kindergarten

Math

- **Number and Number Sense:** Count forward by 5s and 10s, to 30, count backward from 10, identify numbers 0-10, recognizes patterns in numbers count objects, sort objects and explain the sorting rule, organize and display data using bar graphs and pictograph.
- **Exploring Numbers:** Count with whole numbers to 31, identify and create set of objects with more or less, or equal amounts, recognize odd and even number of objects, identify the position of an object using the number first and fifth,
- **Computation and Estimation:** Add and Subtract up to 10 using concrete items.
- **Measurement:** Names coins, and their values, identify, instruments used to measure lengths, weight, time and temperature, tell time by the hour, and compare features of objects.
- **Geometry:** Identify and describe geometric shapes, recognized and describe basic 2 and 3 –dimensional shapes, including circles, triangle, rectangle, pyramid, cube and cylinder.
- **Probability and Statistics:** Count and tally, create picture graphs and tables.
- **Patterns, Functions, and Algebra:** Sort and classify objects, identify and extend patterns

Kindergarten

Science

- **Scientific Investigate, Reasoning and Logic:** Investigate the five senses (hearing, sight, smell, taste and touch).
- **Matter:** Recognize and describes eight basic colors, shapes, textures, relative weight and size, position speed, water and its properties.
- **Life Processes:** Understand the basic needs and processes in plant and animal growth, compare living thing and identify likenesses and differences, describe how specific plant and animals parts help them survive, explain what plant and animals need to survive, classify **living**, nonliving things, and investigate the needs of living things.
- **Earth Patterns, Cycles, and Changes:** Describe patterns and cycles in daily life weathers, home and school routines.
- **Earth/Space:** Investigate how shadows occur, describe the different ways objects move, demonstrate that objects move differently on different surfaces.

Kindergarten

Social Studies

- **History:** Discuss past and present events, describe people honored by holidays and identify people and events by holidays.
- **Geography:** Compare location of things; left to right, up and down, back and front, near and far, use
- **Civics:** Identify patriotic symbols (Statue of Liberty, bald eagle,) recites the Pledge of Allegiance.
- **Economics:** Understand the difference between needs and wants, identify people job.

In kindergarten students learn about themselves, their schools and their communities. By the end of kindergarten student, should have learn:

- Classroom routines

- Follow rules and accept responsibilities to learn and follow the class rules.

- Understand the role of the teacher and principal.

- Members of the school community are responsible for the school environment.

- Understand that people have basic needs and some people have special needs
  For example, some students wear eyeglasses, hearing aids.

- Understand that weather changes with the four seasons.

- Understand that families have different cultures, and responsibilities are shared in
  the family.

- Understand that people have attributes that makes them individuals which
  include; eye, hair color, like and dislikes.

Mathematics

Number and Number Sense: Standard I				
First Grade	Second Grade	Third Grade	Fourth Grade	Fifth Grade
• Understand place value to 100	• Identify place value of 3 digits numbers	• Recognize place value with 6-digit numbers	•Recognize place value through millions	•Recognize commonly used fractions
•Count by 5s, 10s, and 20s,	• Count and perform simple computations with coins	• Identify whether any whole number is even or odd	• Round whole number through millions	•Use whole numbers, fractions, and decimals to represent equivalent forms of the same number
•Identify ½ and ¼	•Proper Fraction (1/2 1/3, ¼ 1.8, 1/10	•Compare the fractions on number line	•Identify and compare fractions	• Prime , factor, multiples
•Count by 2s to 20	•Compare and order whole number 0-999 <. >, =	•Read and write decimals	• Read and write decimals to thousandths	•Compare and order numbers
•Count coins equal 100 cents or less				

Data Analysis and Probability: Standard 2: Students use data collections and analysis, statistics and probability to make valid inferences, decisions, and arguments and to solve a variety of real-world problems.

First Grade	Second Grade	Third Grade	Fourth Grade	Fifth Grade
•Identify and describe various forms of data collection •Interpret information from graphs	•Interpret a simple graph •Record data from experiments	•Construct a bar graph • Interpret bar and picture graphs •Explain the concepts of as chance; ex coin 50/50 of heads or tails	•Determine probability using concrete items • Draw line and bar graphs of collection data	•Construct tree diagrams to determine probability • Collect and display data using stem and leaf plot, line graphs, and bar graphs •Find means and modes of set of data

Pattern, Algebra, And Functions: Standard 3: Students use algebraic methods to explore, model and describe patterns, relationship, and functions involving numbers, shapes, data, and graphs within a variety of real-world problem solving situations.

First Grade	Second Grade	Third Grade	Fourth Grade	Fifth Grade
•Sort and classify objects • Describe, extend, and create patterns	• Create a pattern with symbols and objects • Create word problems	•Recognize, analyze, and extend patterns • Demonstrate and understand of equality	•Recognize and demonstrate meaning of numeric equality •Extend given patterns or tables	•Extend numerical patterns •Describe the concept of variable

Geometry: Standard 4: Students use geometric methods, properties, and relationship as a means to recognize, draw, describe, connect, and analyze shapes and representations in the physical world.

First Grade	Second Grade	Third Grade	Fourth Grade	Fifth Grade
●Describe proximity of objects. ●Draw, describe, and sort geometric shapes	●Identify and compare plane and solid geometric shape (square, triangle, rectangular solid, cylinder, cone ●Demonstrate an understanding of symmetry	●Identify properties of solid and plane figure ●Draw congruent and symmetrical figures ●Identify and draw line segments and angles	●Identify and illustrate, points, lines segments, rays, and angles ●Identify and draw lines that are intersecting, parallel, and perpendicular ●Locate points on a coordinate plane	●Classify angles(right, obtuse, acute) ●Measure and draw angles and triangle

Measurement and Discrete Mathematics: Standard 5: Student make and use direct and indirect measurements, metric and U.S. customary, to describe and compare the real world and to prepare for student for discrete functions, fractals and chaos which have evolved in the age of technology.

First Grade	Second Grade	Third Grade	Fourth Grade	Fifth Grade
●Count and compare coin ●Tell time to the nearest half hour ●Measure length and height ●Compare weight of 2 objects	●Count, write and recognize Money up to $2.00 ●Tell time to the quarter hour ●Use language appropriately ●Compare measurement ●Estimate and measure length, area, volume and mass	●Count change up to $5.00 ●Tell time to the nearest 5 minutes ●Identify equivalent period of time ●Read temperature to the nearest degree ●Measure using US Customary and metric units	●Estimate and measure using customary units ●Estimate and measure using metric units ●Convert customary and metric units ●Find perimeter with customary and metric units	●Determine perimeter of polygons ●Determine area of square, rectangle, and triangles ●Solve problems using appropriate units of measure

Computation and Estimation: Standard 6: The students use both inductive and deductive reasoning as they make conjectures and test the validity or arguments

First Grade	Second Grade	Third Grade	Fourth Grade	Fifth Grade
•Solve story and picture problems with addition and subtraction	• Create and solve one step addition and subtraction problems • Recall basic addition and subtraction facts • Estimate sums and differences • Understand inverse relationship of addition and subtractions	•Add and subtract 4-digit whole numbers •Recall basic multiplication and divisions facts •Add and subtract fractions with like denominations •Add and subtract decimals	•Add and subtract whole numbers •Multiple 3-digit by 2-digit numbers •Complete divisions of a whole number by a 1-digit divisor •Estimate answers for whole numbers when performing basic operation(+,-,x ÷) •Add and subtract fractions with like and unlike denominators	•Create and solve problems involving whole numbers using +, _, x,÷) •Multiply and divide two numbers expresses as decimals • Divide a 4-digit number by a 2-digit number •Add and subtract with fraction and mixed numerals

The aim of the charts above is to show the major mathematics topics that are focued on in grades first to fifth. Different math curricula utilize different scope and sequence, plus states standards might vary. The charts are an overview of what students should know and be able to do by the end of each grade. The mathematics curriculum at each grades level is organized into units of instruction. The following resources that parents should always visit to understand the curriculum in more detail are: Department Curriculum for Mathematics at their child school. Sites recommended by: National Council of Teacher Mathematics.
http://Illuminations.nctm.org/; http://archives.math.utk,edu/topics/; www.eduplace.com/math/brain/;www.figurethis.org/;www.ed.gov/pubs/parents/Math/;wwww.multiplication.com/parents.htm; www.aaamath.com/index.html

English

Oral Language				
First Grade	**Second Grade**	**Third Grade**	**Fourth Grade**	**Fifth Grade**
• Tell and retell stories in logical order •Express ideas in complete sentences •Initiate conversation •Follow the rules from conversation •Count syllables in words (up to 3) •Create rhyming words orally	•Use correct verb tenses in oral communication •Give and follow oral direction in 3 or 4 steps • Participate as a contributor and leader in groups	•Use effective communications skills •Present brief oral reports	•Use grammatically correct language • Give and listen to oral reports	•Listen, draw conclusions, and share responses •Use effective nonverbal communications •Planned and make oral presentations

Writing

	Reading			
First Grade	**Second Grade**	**Third Grade**	**Fourth Grade**	**Fifth Grade**
●Use beginning and ending consonant vowel sound to decode words ● Reread and self correct ● Read familiar stories ●Answer questions about what is read ● Identify the main idea ●Use a picture dictionary ●Comment and write about what is read ●Alphabetize using first letter	●Use phonetic clues when reading ●Use pictures and meaning clues when reading ●Use prefixes and suffixes ●Identify story sequences ●Use reading strategies to study a variety of fiction, nonfiction and poetry ●Retell what is read ●Use a table of contents and an index ●Use a dictionary	● Use work analysis skills when reading ●Read folk tales, biographies, legend, fables, and poetry ●Demonstrate reading comprehension of fiction and nonfiction ● Use dictionaries, thesauruses, and glossaries correctly ●Comprehend information from a variety of print resources	●Read and learn unfamiliar words, using context to clarify ●Explain words with multiple meanings ●Compare fact and fantasy in historical fiction ● Explain the author's purpose ●Paraphrase what is read ●Identify major events and supporting details ●Use information sources to research topic	●Read fiction and non-fiction with fluency and accuracy ●Use root words, or prefixes, and suffixes to understand unfamiliar words ●Describe character development in fiction and poetry ●Describe plot and conflict resolution ●Read a variety of literary forms ●Demonstrate Comprehension about reading ●Skim materials to locate information ●Develop charts, maps, and graphs

First Grade	Second Grade	Third Grade	Fourth Grade	Fifth Grade
●Organize ideas for writing ●Write to communication ●Focus on one topics ●Spell frequently used word correctly ●Use complete sentences	●Write stories, letter, and simple explanations ●Organize writing with a beginning, middle, and end ●Use different types of sentence ●Correctly spell frequently used words ●Use basics computer skills ●Make transition to cursive handwriting	●Write descriptive paragraphs ●Use expand sentences in writings ●Write stories, letter, spelling, explanations, and short punctuation ●Revise and edit writings ●Write legibly in cursive	●Compose effective narrative and explanations ●Write several related paragraphs on a single topics ●Edit and revise work	●Write to describe, inform, entertain, and explain ●Choose planning strategies for writing ●Vary sentence structure ●Edit and revise work for correct grammar, capitalization, spelling, punctuation, and sentence structure.

Reading/ Language Art/ Resource for parents: National Council of Teacher of English, www. ncte.org/parents; www.reading.org;www.angelfire.com/wi/writingprocess/; www.ed.gov/pubs/ CompactforReading;http://grammar.ccc.commnet.edu/gramma; www.udel.edu/ETL/RWN/Activities.html

Science

Scientific Investigation, Reasoning and Logic				
First Grade	**Second Grade**	**Third Grade**	**Fourth Grade**	**Fifth Grade**
●Conduct investigation using the senses and simple instruments	●Plan and conduct investigations ●Classify items according to like characteristics	●Plan and conduct investigations	● Plan and conduct investigation	●Plan conduct investigation

Force, Motion and Energy

First Grade	Second Grade	Third Grade	Fourth Grade	Fifth Grade
• Understand that objects exhibit different kinds of motion	•Investigation characteristics of magnets	•Investigation and understand simple machines	•Investigate and understand the interaction of moving objects •Investigate the characteristics of electricity	•Investigate sound •Investigate characteristics of visible light

Matter/Life Processes

First Grade	Second Grade	Third Grade	Fourth Grade	Fifth Grade
•Investigation how materials interact with water	•Investigate solids, liquids, and gases •Understand changes in matter	•Investigation and understand physical properties	**Life Processes** •Identify basic plant anatomy and life processes	•Understand matter and the effect of temperature on its various states
Life Processes •Identify the parts, needs and characteristics of plant and animal	**Life Processes** •Understand plant and animals life cycles	**Life Processes** •Investigate adaption of animals •Identify instinct and learned behaviors of animals		

Living Systems

First Grade	Second Grade	Third Grade	Fourth Grade	Fifth Grade
•**Understand the difference between living organism and non-living organisms**	•Describe how living organisms are interdependent •Understand that habitats change overtime	•Understand relationships in food chains •Investigate different environment (water, and land biomes)	•Understand plant and animal interactions in the ecosystem	•Investigate the characteristics of organisms: vertebrates and invertebrates; vascular and nonvascular plants •Identify the five kingdoms of living things •Describe the parts of a cell and their functions

Earth/Space Systems

Earth/Space Systems				
First Grade	**Second Grade**	**Third Grade**	**Fourth Grade**	**Fifth Grade**
●Describe the basic relationship between the sun and the Earth	●Investigate And understand weather patterns	●nvestigate the major components of soil	●Describe weather conditions and phenomena ●Learn about tools used to predict weather	●Describe the ocean environment

Earth Patterns, Cycles, and Changes

First Grade	Second Grade	Third Grade	Fourth Grade	Fifth Grade
●Understand seasonal changes and their impact on life	●Describe how weather affects the environment	●Investigate cycles in nature such as day/night, seasons, and tides	●Investigate the relationships of the Earth, moon, and the sun	●Understand Earth's changes surface: Fossils Human impact Identification of rock types Plate tectonics weathering and erosion

Resource for parents: National Science Association: www.nsta.org; www.nsta.org/explore; www.ed.gov/pubd/parents/Science/index.html

The History and Social Standards for K-5 are taught in different combinations and sequences depending on the state and the school.

First Grade	Second Grade	Third Grade
History	**History**	**History**
●Interpret picture time lines to show past/present ●Describe contributions of American leaders George Washington, Ben Franklin, Abraham Lincoln, George Washington Carver ●Discuss people and events associated with holidays	●Identify contributions of Egypt and China ●Compare lives and contributions of American Indians ●Compare changes in community life over time	●Identify contributions of ancient Rome and Greece ●Study the West African empire of Mali ●Understand cause and effect relationship in history
Geography	**Geography**	**Geography**
●Recognize map symbols and use cardinal directions (North, South. East, West on globes and map legends ●Make s simple map	●Locate China and Egypt on maps and globes ●Use maps to locate Native American regions ●Describe regional climate and adaptations of living things ●Locate the equator, seven continents, and four oceans on maps and globes ●Local selected rivers, mountain ranges, and lakes on US maps ●Make a map including title, legend, and compass rose	●Locate Greece, Rome, West Africa, Spain, England, and Frances on world maps ●Identify equator, prime meridian, four hemispheres, seven continent, and four ocean, ●Identify exploration routes in the Americas ●Use letter-number grid system on maps to find locations ●Interpret geographic information from maps, tables, graphs, and charts

The goals of any schools systems are to have a curriculum that shows what students know and what they are expected to learn at different grade levels. The tables in this guide are basic from the State Department of Education of Virginia, Maryland along with the National Standard of Teacher for Mathematics, English, Science and Social Studies. This guide is to give parents ideas of what is taught at different grade levels. As stated early it is very important for parents to take the time to visit your child's state and local school system website so that you will have a better understand of what your child will be expected to learn occurring to their school systems at different grade levels. Remember this is a guide each state curriculum is different in some way, but remember all school systems have the same goal, which is to foster an environment where all children can learn and be successful.

CHAPTER 6
Transition to Middle and High School

The middle school years and high school years can be filled with all sorts of bumps along the way. Middle school is the time parents tend to be less involved, but it's the time your child needs you the most for encouragement and guidance. This is the time that children are growing up and a world where most parents expected their child to go to college, and most students have those same goals. Middle school is the time for parents and students to start planning for college. Parents must be vocal about what your child needs are. Parents should always feel comfortable calling your child's school to say, I think my son or daughter needs extra help because he or she is falling math; or do you have rigorous classes for my child because they are doing well in some areas such as English or Science classes.

Research is clear; students who take Algebra and Geometry by the eighth grade are most likely to go to college than those who don't. These math classes are required to take more advance classes in high school and to take science classes like Chemistry and Physics. In addition to taking math ever year in middle school your child should take: English each year, History including geography and science; Foreign Language many colleges require at least two years of a language which your child can begin in middle school. The transition from elementary to middle or junior high school takes places as early as the fifth grade and sometime sixth grade, either way it can be a tough transition because of some many changes from the cozy elementary school setting. Children need strong preparation in middle school to take the high school classes that are required for college. The bottom line is that students will needed more than just the basic high school graduation requirements to be prepared and successful in college. Prepared for college must starts early as elementary and middle school; if not the students won't be prepared for high school or college.

During adolescent years child undergo significantly physical and emotional changes. Middle school is a crucial point in the lifetime of learning. While elementary and middle school focused on the student, high school solidifies skills and middle school is the beginning of when student learn the importance of education. Depending on your child's school district middle school can begin at the end of fifth or sixth grades. The courses that your child takes in middle school lay the foundation for high school. If your child has a strong educational foundation in middle school they will be able to take college credits courses in high school. Advanced Placement (AP) and honor classes in high school put students at an advantage when applying for college.

Classes for Grade 6-8

Grade 6	Grade 7	Grade8
English	English	English
Math	Math	Math
Science	Science	Science
Social Studies	Social Studies	Social Studies
Foreign Language	Foreign Language	Foreign Language

• Make sure that the English classes offer grammar, writing and literature

• For math know whether your child has masted the basic math skills. If possible try to have your child take Algebra I in the eighth grade, make sure that the child is ready for the class. Listen to your child's teacher, your child, and especially know your child's test scores in math. The level that your child reads on is very important, so you must also know your child's reading level. As parents you should reassure, encourage and support. Responding to your child's educational and personal needs to build a foundation one must give support at home, school and most of all as a parent you should know how to communicate with your child.

Home	School
• Established routine for your child to study	• Attending school activities
• Have a calendar of school event	• Know your child's teacher and the school administrators
• Calendar to track assignments	• Contact teacher don't wait for them to contact you
• Respect the student effort	• Monitor your child's progress by staying in touch with your child teachers
• Provide help when needed	• Understand school policies, particularly how they apply to student evaluation, the grading system and the requirement for graduation.
• Emphasize the importance of school with actions and words.	• Stay informed by reading the school newsletter, visited the school website.

Communication: Some parents and students have trouble communicate with each others. It doesn't' have to be, here are several way that might help:\

• Find time to talk, and listen to each other; at meals time, watching TV, in the car
• Talk about responsible behavior and risk taking
• Listen to your child and do not judge
• Be honest
• Ask your child about certain issues
• Be a good role model
• Always ask you child what they think when you are communicating with each other because you learn more.
• Spend time together with your child by watching TV; participate in your child's activities; as a parent one must support your child's interests.

As a parent your expectations have a huge influence on what your child expects of himself or herself, even if they don't want you to know. During the middle school years students need help with management skills and with strategies on how to deal with the additional work load. Without help from parents students can feel and become overwhelmed. When students move to middle school they are faced with a whole different set of grading criteria, many new teachers, and a new environment. During this time, students require a lot of support from parents, teachers, friends, and family. Middle school is a much large environment and it is important that parents have some ideas as what to expect at the middle school grade.

5th Grade

5th grader students will be assigned book reports, lab reports, and other projects that demand concentration, concrete organized skills and sustained effort. 5th grader seeks and retains more information. Many of the facts will stay with them for the rest of their life. Here are some examples by subject, what student will learn.

Language Arts	Math and Science	Social Studies
●Group activities cooperative learning ●Use increase memory capacity to strengthen spelling skills ●Engage in independent often voracious reading ●Write rudimentary research papers ● Read and memorize poetry	●Familiarize with the human body ●Classification systems such as the periodic table ●Analyze through repeat experiments and control variables. ●Work with decimals and double-digits divisions ●Collect data using various measurement tools ●Use computer	●Memorize state capitals, president, and other facts ●Focus on geography and world's natural resources.

6th Grade

The 6th grade student thinks that the world is meant to be picked apart by asking questions. In the classroom worksheets are replace for more challenge and open-ended assignments. Tasks are focus more on interpretation rather than rote memorization. This is the time that students pursue activities like foreign language, music and art which helps to shape their character.

Language Arts	Math and Science	Social Studies
●Read non-fiction history books, especially biographies ●Conduct interviews for research ●Learn how to read and compose footnotes and bibliographies	●Untangle complicated word problems ●Learn about probability, statistics and percentage ●Format number using scientific notation	●Engage more closely with ideas by using primary documents ●Consider world events through various perspectives ●Complete current events assignments

7th Grade

In the 7th grade this is the beginning when adolescents deal with mood swings, identify crises and social drama. The school work of the 7th grader transition into adulthood through tasks that demand reaching out and connecting with society. Although 7th graders sometime act unpredictably, they will begin to show patience and maturity through collaboration inside and outside the classroom.

Language Arts	Math and Science	Social Studies
●Read longer book, many that involved issues of fairness ●Learn to write essay ●Discuss literary elements of books in detail about setting, character, plot, and themes ●Acquire a rich and varied vocabulary	●Interprets charts and graphs ●Explore the microscope world ●Solve problems involving decimals, fraction, percent, and geometry ●Study pattern and sequences ●Utilize geometrical tools like the compass and protractor ●Begin learning algebra, the concept of zero, and integers	●Lesson on the environment, historical conflicts, and ethics increase on politics and social issues ●Exhibit early stages of abstract reasoning

No getting around it, 8th grader rebels passionately and frequently, teachers try to channel this behavior by giving students assignments that give the students the opportunity to make decisions about his life and identity. More than ever 8th grader grapples with what makes them unique. They insist that school is boring and they purport to know everything, however they are open to academic challenge.

8th

Language Arts	Math and Science	Social Science
●Construct lengthier , more structured research reports ●Experiment with the different purpose of writing ●Use literature and writing to express and understand themselves ●Explore aesthetic techniques in literature	●Become interested in psychology and questions about themselves ●Interpret a greater range of graphical representations ●Solve basic algebra equations with unknown ●Inquire about technology and how things work	●Discuss how current events relate to various studies ●Investigate solutions for the world's problems ●Demonstrate an interest different culture

When children move up and out of elementary school as parents one can not assume that they are able to handle these changes without the help of parents. The middle school year and especially high school years are challenging years and this is the time that requires extra support from mom and dad.

One of the biggest milestones in a child's life is the milestone from middle school to high school. When students enter high school they are looking forward to making new friends, however, they are also concerned about being picked on or teased by older students. As many students make the transition into high school, many experience a decline in grades and attendance (Barone, Aguirre-Deandreis, &Trickett, 1991); they view themselves more negatively and experience the need for more friends (Hertzog, et.al, 1996) and by the end of the 10th grade, as many as 6% drop out of school(Owings & Peng,1992). According to Phelan, and Yu, & Davidson, (1994), middle school students and those who have been labeled gifted and talented the transition to high school can be and unpleasant experience. The beginning of high school years is when parents and students plan out the courses which a child should take year after year. This is done so that the children meet the state requirements to graduate from high school. Each state has it own requirements for graduation from high school. Additional course work might be needed for students to be accepted or enroll at a specific college or universities.

Middle school students want to know what high school is going to be like, it is very important that parents understand how programs and procedures work in high school. Parents need to be actively involved by communication with their eight-graders by decisions what classes they will take in the ninth grade. According to Mac Iver (1990), a high school transition program should includes a variety of activities that (1) provide students and parents with information about the new school (2) provide students with social support during the transition, and (3) bring middle school and high school staff together to learn the curriculum and requirements. Underlying successful high school transition programs are activities that bring middle school and high school administrators, counselors, and teacher together to learn about programs, courses, curriculum, and requirements (Hertzog, et.al., 1996; Vars, 1998).

The importance of parents being involved in their child's transition from middle to high school can hardly be overestimated. Parents should have a clear understanding of high school procedures. At the middle school level, teachers and administrators should inform parents about transition activities at the high school. Parents should meet with their high school counselor to discuss course work, schedules visits to the high school with their child in the spring or fall; spend a day at the high school to help their child understand the high school curriculum. In planning for high school classes parent should understand the following the curriculum and requirements occurring to the states:

●*English: Most states require that a student has four credits in English. Composition, writing and literature are generally included in these credits.*

●*History: Most states require at least three credits in history/social science. This generally includes American History and World History. Additional half credits can be earned in economics and government, other credits could include course in European History.*

●*Mathematics: Most states require three credits in Math, these credits generally included Algebra I, Geometry, Algebra II, Trigonometry, Applied Math, Advanced Math, Pre-Calculus, Calculus or Business Math. Since the NCLB Act most state requires that the math classes are Algebra I, Geometry and Algebra II.*

•Science: Most states require three credits in Science these credits generally included Biology, Chemistry, Physical Science, Physics, or an elective Science.

•Elective Credits: The elective credits that a students selected should be based upon the student future goals. For example is a student planning to pursue a college degree the student will need credits in Fine Arts, and foreign language. If the students are planning a vocational track, the student should take courses which will facilitate their particular track. College and vocational schools should be researched because certain colleges require that a student has two years in one particular language while other college may require two credits in foreign language are not the same. Students who take AP classes can earned both high school and college credit. Remembered that high school is the begin stage that helps students set goals for the rest of their life.

All in all, when your child moves from middle school to high school don't assume that they can handle this alone, parents who have open communication with their child, that student will stand a better chance of making the transition. Support your child, without doing to much for them. All parents want their child to be successful in school and in life. There are many ways to help your child achieve. Below is a list of things parents can do to help their child:

•Set expectations for your child

•Make clear that school is their first priority

•Volunteer at your child's school

•Know your child's schedule at school

•Communicate regular with your child's teacher about their progress

•At home teach your child how to study: Identify a comfortable place to study; make sure they have all the materials they need; make sure they know the difference between doing homework, reviewing homework and studying for exams.

•Encourage them to study in a quiet (Check in their room to see if they are studying).

•Make sure they know how to use different resources Internet, and the Media Center to help with writing research papers.

•Good Nutrition

•Help teens manger their time, which includes making sure they allocate time for sleep and rest as part of their daily routine.

- Communicate about school and their classes.
- Progress Log

To:_____

From_____

Date_____

Re: Academic Progress of _____ is a student in your ____
_____ class. As a parent(s) we are monitoring my student's progress. We need some
information from you in order to help my child. Please return this for to the student.

Is the student's performance in your class satisfactory? Yes _____ No _____

Current Grade: A_____ B_____ C_____ D_____ E/F_____

Please check all that apply:

	Poor/test quiz grade
	Missing Home work How Many _____
	Does not complete Homework
	Poor organization skills
	Not prepared for class
	Distractive/inattentive
	Insufficient academic background for class
	Excessive absences
	Behavioral issues
	Does not make up work
	Number of tests failed
	Number of quizzes failed
	Number of missed class work How many?

- Log for quizzes and tests per subjects, most teachers announce the dates.

- Know if the teacher gives pop quizzes and test.

• Always read the teacher course outline; or the local school system requirement for each class that your child is taking in school.

• Understand the mathematics Curriculum from Grade 7-12

Each school systems have their own track for their mathematics programs; this is an example of how a track could be. As a parent visit your child's school website and talk to your child's counselor and math teacher about the math curriculum. This is a possible track which might be difference from your child school.

	7th	8th	9th	10th	11th	12th
College Level 1	Math 7	Algebra I	Geometry	Algebra II	Pre Calculus AP Statistics	Calculus
Level 2	Math 7	Pre-Algebra	Algebra I	Geometry	Algebra II	Pre-Calculus AP Statistics
Honor	Honor Alg I	Honor Geometry	Honor Alg II	Honor Pre Calculus	Calculus	Calculus III

• Get to know your child learning styles

Types of Learning Styles

Visual	Children in this category understand and remember concepts better if their educational materials come with a graph, pictures, or allow them to associate concepts with a visual scenario. The use of a computer and drawing can help promote learning for a visual learner.
Auditory	Children in this category prefer to listen to lesson rather than reading or writing. Their brain can retain information well if they hear it or if the information is in the form of a rhyme or made into a song. As children we learn the alphabet this way.

Tactile or Kinesthetic	Learners in this category understand and remember information better if they talk about it to other people. They often need to make physical contact with things they are learning. A child that kinesthetic learner usually find it difficult to sit for a long period of time and prefers to constantly be on the move. Hand on activities and experiments can be beneficial to the kinesthetic learners.

•MULTIPLE INTELLIGENCES

The Multiple Intelligence theory suggests that no one set of teaching strategies will work best for all students at all times. All children have different proclivities in the seven intelligences, so any particular strategy is likely to be successful with several students, and yet, not for others. Because of these individual differences among students, teachers are best advised to use a broad range of teaching strategies with their students. As long as instructors shift their intelligence emphasis from presentation to presentation, there will always be a time during the period or day when a student has his or her own highly developed intelligence(s) actively involved in learning. Source of all the Multiple Intelligences (Armstrong, 2000).

Key Points in MI Theory

- Each person possesses all seven intelligences - MI theory is not a "type theory" for determining the one intelligence that fits. It is a theory of cognitive functioning, and it proposed that each person has capacities in all seven intelligences.

- Most people can develop each intelligence to an adequate level of competency - although an individual may bewail his deficiencies in a given area and consider his problems innate and intractable, Gardner suggests that virtually everyone has the capacity to develop all seven intelligences to a reasonably high level of performance if given the appropriate encouragement, enrichment, and instruction.

- Intelligences usually work together in complex ways - Gardner points out that each intelligence as described above is actually a "fiction"; that is no intelligence exists by itself in life (except perhaps in very rare instances in savants and brain-injured individuals.) Intelligences are always interacting with each other.

- There are many ways to be intelligent within each category - there is no standard set of attributes that one must have to be considered intelligent in a specific area. Consequently, a person may not be able to read, yet be highly linguistic because he can tell a terrific story or has a large, oral vocabulary. Similarly, a person may be quite awkward on the playing field, yet possess superior bodily-kinesthetic intelligence when she weaves a carpet or creates an inlaid chess table. MI theory emphasizes the rich diversity of ways in which people show their gifts within intelligences as well as between intelligences.

MULTIPLE INTELLIGENCES TEST

Where does your true intelligence lie? This quiz will tell you where you stand and what to do about it. Read each statement. If it expresses some characteristic of yours and sounds true for the most part, jot down a "T." If it doesn't, mark an "F." If the statement is sometimes true, sometimes false, leave it blank.

1. _____ I'd rather draw a map than give someone verbal directions.

2. _____ I can play (or used to play) a musical instrument.

3. _____ I can associate music with my moods.

4. _____ I can add or multiply in my head.

5. _____ I like to work with calculators and computers.

6. _____ I pick up new dance steps fast.

7. _____ It's easy for me to say what I think in an argument or debate.

8. _____ I enjoy a good lecture, speech or sermon.

9. _____ I always know north from south no matter where I am.

10. _____ Life seems empty without music.

11. _____ I always understand the directions that come with new gadgets or appliances.

12. _____ I like to work puzzles and play games.

13. _____ Learning to ride a bike (or skates) was easy.

14. _____ I am irritated when I hear an argument or statement that sounds illogical.

15. _____ My sense of balance and coordination is good.

16. _____ I often see patterns and relationships between numbers faster and easier than others.

17. _____ I enjoy building models (or sculpting).

18. _____ I'm good at finding the fine points of word meanings.

19. _____ I can look at an object one way and see it sideways or backwards just as easily.

20. _____ I often connect a piece of music with some event in my life.

21. _____ I like to work with numbers and figures.

22. _____ Just looking at shapes of buildings and structures is pleasurable to me.

23. _____ I like to hum, whistle and sing in the shower or when I'm alone.

24. _____ I'm good at athletics.

25. _____ I'd like to study the structure and logic of languages.

26. _____ I'm usually aware of the expression on my face.

27. _____ I'm sensitive to the expressions on other people's faces.

28. _____ I stay "in touch" with my moods.   I have no trouble identifying them.

29. _____ I am sensitive to the moods of others.

30. _____ I have a good sense of what others think of

MULTIPLE INTELLIGENCE SCORING SHEET

Place a check mark by each item you marked as "true." Add your totals.   A total of four in any of the categories A through E indicates strong ability.   In categories F and G a score of one or more means you have abilities as well.

A	B	C	D	E	F	G
Linguistic	Logical-Mathematical	Musical	Spatial	Bodily-Kinesthetic	Intra-personal	Inter-personal
7 ___	4 ___	2 ___	1 ___	6 ___	26 ___	27 ___
8 ___	5 ___	3 ___	9 ___	13 ___	28 ___	29 ___
14 ___	12 ___	10 ___	11 ___	15 ___		30 ___
18 ___	16 ___	20 ___	19 ___	17 ___		
25 ___	21 ___	23 ___	22 ___	24 ___		
Totals: ___	___	___	___	___	___	___

The Seven Multiple Intelligences in Children

Children who are strongly:	Think	Love	Need
Linguistic	in words	reading, writing, telling stories, playing word games, etc.	books, tapes, writing tools paper diaries, dialogues, discussion, debate stories
Logical-Mathematical	by reasoning	experimenting, questioning, figuring out puzzles, calculating, etc.	things to explore and think about, science materials, manipulatives, trips to the planetarium and science museum
Spatial	in images and pictures	designing, drawing, visualizing, doodling, etc.	art, LEGOs, video, movies, slides, imagination games, mazes, puzzles, illustrated books, trips to art museums
Bodily-Kinesthetic	through somatic sensations	dancing, running, jumping, building, touching, gesturing, etc.	role play, drama, movement, things to build, sports and physical games, tactile experiences, hands-on learning
Musical	via rhythms and melodies	singing, whistling, humming, tapping feet and hands, listening, etc..	sing-along time, trips to concerts, music playing at home and school, musical instruments
Interpersonal	by bouncing ideas off other people	leading, organizing, relating, manipulating, mediating, partying, etc.	friends, group games, social gatherings, community events, clubs, mentors/apprenticeships
Intrapersonal	deeply inside themselves	setting goals, meditating, dreaming, being quiet,	secret places, time alone, self-paced projects, choices

CHECKLIST FOR ASSESSING STUDENTS' MULTIPLE INTELLIGENCES

Name of Student: _____

In each of the following categories, check all items that apply.

Linguistic Intelligence

_____writes better than average for age

_____spins tall tales or tells jokes and stories

_____has a good memory for names, places, dates, or trivia

_____enjoys word games

_____enjoys reading books

_____spells words accurately (preschool: does developmental spelling that is advanced for age)

_____appreciates nonsense rhymes, puns, tongue twisters, etc.

_____enjoys listening to the spoken word (stories, commentary on the radio, talking, books)

_____has a good vocabulary for age

_____communicates to others in a highly verbal way

Other Linguistic Strengths:

Logical-Mathematical Intelligence

_____ asks a lot of questions about how things work

_____ computes arithmetic problems in his/her head quickly (preschool: math concepts are advanced for age)

_____enjoys math class (preschool: enjoys counting and doing other things with number)

_____finds math computer games interesting (no exposure to computers: enjoys other math or counting games)

_____enjoys playing chess, checkers, or other strategy games (preschool: board games requiring counting squares)

_____enjoys working on logic puzzles or brain teasers (preschool: enjoys hearing logical nonsense such as in Alice's Adventures in Wonderland)

_____enjoys putting things in categories or hierarchies

_____likes to experiment in a way that shows higher order cognitive thinking processes

_____thinks on a more abstract or conceptual level than peers

_____has a good sense of cause-effect for age

Other Logical-Mathematical Strengths:

Spatial Intelligence

_____reports clear visual images

_____reads maps, charts, and diagrams more easily that text (preschool: enjoys visuals more than text)

_____daydreams more than peers

_____enjoys art activities

_____draws figures that are advanced for age

_____likes to view movies, slides, or other visual presentations

_____enjoys doing puzzles, mazes, Where's Waldo? or similar visual activities

_____builds interesting three-dimensional constructions for age (e.g., LEGO buildings)

_____gets more out of pictures than words while reading

_____doodles on workbooks, worksheets, or other materials

Other Spatial Strengths:

Bodily-Kinesthetic Intelligence

_____excels in one or more sports (preschool: shows physical prowress advanced for age)

_____moves, twitches, taps, or fidgets while seated for a long time in one spot

_____cleverly mimics other people's gestures or mannerisms

_____loves to take things apart and put them back together again

_____put his/her hands all over something he/she's just seen

_____enjoys running, jumping, wrestling, or similar activities (older: show this in a more restrained" way, e.g., woodworking, sewing, mechanics) or good fine-motor coordination in other ways

_____has a dramatic way of expressing himself/herself

_____reports different physical sensations while thinking or working

_____enjoys working with clay or other tactile experiences (e.g., finger-painting)

Other Bodily-Kinesthetic Strengths:

Musical Intelligence

_____tells you when music sounds off-key or disturbing in some way other way

_____remembers melodies of songs

_____has a good singing voice

_____plays a musical instrument or sings in choir or other group (preschool: enjoys playing percussion instruments and/or singing in a group)

_____has a rhythmic way of speaking and/or moving

_____unconsciously hums to himself/herself

_____taps rhythmically on the table or desks as he/she works

_____sensitive to environmental noises (e.g., rain on the roof)

Other Musical Strengths:

Interpersonal Intelligence

_____enjoys socializing with peers

_____seems to be a natural leader

_____gives advice to friends who have problems

_____seems to be street smart

_____belongs to clubs, committees, or other group organizations (preschool: seems to be part of a general education social group)

_____enjoys informally teaching other kids

_____likes to play games with other kids

_____has two or more close friends

_____has a good sense of empathy or concern for others

_____others seek out his/her empathy or concern for others

_____others seek out his/her company

Other Interpersonal Strengths:

Intrapersonal Intelligence

_____displays a sense of independence or a strong will

_____has a realistic sense of his/her strengths and weaknesses _____does well when left alone or to play or study

_____marches to the beat of a different drummer in his/her style of living and learning

_____has an interest or hobby that he/she doesn't talk much about

_____has a good sense of self-direction

_____prefers working alone to working with others

_____accurately expresses how he/she is feeling

_____is able to learn from his/her failures and successes in life

_____has high self-esteem

Other Intrapersonal Strengths:

Excerpted from Armstrong, Thomas. *Multiple Intelligences in the Classroom,* Alexandria, Virginia, Association for Supervision and Curriculum Development (2000).

MULTIPLE INTELLIGENCES: STRATEGIES IN THE CLASSROOM

The following list provides a survey of the techniques and materials that can be employed in teaching through the multiple intelligences.

Linguistic Intelligence

- lectures, debates

- large- and small-group discussions

- books, worksheets, manuals

- brainstorming

- writing activities

- word games

- sharing time

- storytelling, speeches, reading to class

- •talking books and cassettes

- •extemporaneous speaking

- •journal keeping

- •choral reading

- •individualized reading

- •memorizing linguistic facts

- •tape recording one's words

- •using word processors

- •publishing (e.g., creating class newspapers)

Logical-Mathematical Intelligence

- •mathematical problems on the board

- •Socratic questioning

- •scientific demonstrations

- •logical problem-solving exercises

- •creating codes

- •logic puzzles and games

- •classifications and categorizations

- •quantifications and calculations

- •computer programming languages

- •science thinking

- •logical-sequential presentation of subject matter

- •Piagetian cognitive stretching exercises

- •Heuristic

Spatial Intelligence

- •charts, graphs, diagrams, and maps

- •visualization

- •photography

- videos, slides, and movies

- visual puzzles and mazes

- 3-D construction kits

- art appreciation

- imaginative storytelling

- picture metaphors

- creative daydreaming

- painting, collage, visual arts

- idea sketching

- visual thinking exercises

- graphic symbols

- using mind-maps and other visual organizers

- computer graphics software

- visual awareness activities

- optical illusions

- color cues

- telescopes, microscopes, and binoculars

- visual awareness activities

- draw-and-paint/computer- assisted-design software

- picture literacy experiences

Bodily-Kinesthetic Intelligence

- creative movement, mime

- hands-on thinking

- field trips

- the classroom teacher

- competitive and cooperative games

- physical awareness and relaxation exercises

•all hands-on activities

•crafts

•body maps

•use of kinesthetic imagery

•cooking, gardening, and other "messy" activities

•manipulatives

•virtual reality software

•kinesthetic concepts

•physical education activities

•communicating with body language/ hand signals

•tactile materials and experiences

•body answers

Musical Intelligence

•musical concepts

•singing, humming, whistling

•playing recorded music

•playing live music on piano, guitar, or other instruments

•group singing

•mood music

•music appreciation

•playing percussion instruments

•rhythms, songs, raps, chants

•using background music

•linking old tunes with concepts

•discographies

•creating new melodies for concepts

•listening to inner musical imagery

- •music software

- •supermemory music

Interpersonal Intelligence

- •cooperative groups

- •interpersonal interaction

- •conflict mediation

- •peer teaching

- •board games

- •cross-age tutoring

- •group brainstorming sessions

- •peer sharing

- •community involvement

- •apprenticeships

- •simulations

- •academic clubs

- •interactive software

- •parties / social gatherings as context for learning

- •people sculpting

Intrapersonal Intelligence

- •independent study

- •feeling-toned moments

- •self-paced instruction

- •individualized projects and games

- •private spaces for study

- •one-minute reflection periods

- •interest centers

- •personal connections

•options for homework

•choice time

•self-teaching programmed instruction

•exposure to inspirational/ motivational curricula

•self-esteem activities

•journal keeping

•goal setting sessions

Excerpted from Armstrong, T. *Multiple Intelligences In The Classroom*. Alexandria, VA: Association for Supervision and Curriculum Development (2000).

Parents show a preference for on of the above learning styles, however it is important to remember that your own learning styles may not be the same as your child's. This may be difficult, but what important is for you to try to help your child. Understanding both your own and your child learning styles is important in understanding your child better and will assist you in reinforcing the skills that he or she needs to succeed in school. Once you recognized how your child learns, you will be able to adapt the learning activities to help with homework, study for quizzes and tests and most of all this will also help prevent your child from neither feeling the frustration of nor performing at their best academically and can improve your child's accomplishments and sense of achievements. Your goal as a parent is to find a school that meets your child's needs, but how do you choose between public and private school. What the difference? The table below is a compares of: Private vs. Public Schools

	Public School	Private School
Cost	Public schools cannot charge tuition. Funded through federal, state and local taxes. When you pay taxes, you are paying for your child's education and other children in the community.	Private schools do not receive tax revenue, but instead funded through tuition, fundraising, donations and grants. Parochial schools generally charge less according to the National Catholic Educational Association in their annual statistical report in 2005-2006.
Admissions	Public schools admit *all children.* By law, public school must educate all children, including students with special needs.	Private school are selective they are not obligated to accept every child, and in many private schools admission is very competitive.

Governance	Public schools must follow all federal, state, and local laws in educating children. This laws usually included specific about funding, programs, and the curriculum.	Private school are not subject to the limitations of state education budgets and have more freedom in designing curriculum and instruction.
Curriculum	Public schools offer a general program designed for all children which included math, English, reading, science, history, social studies, physical education, Fine Arts. In the public schools the substance of what children will learn and be able to do is mandated by the state and learning is measured by state standardized tests.	Private schools have the flexibility to create a specialized program for students. Private school can created their own curriculum and assessment systems, although many also choose to use some form of standardized tests.
Teachers	All teachers in a public school must be highly qualified according to the NCLB Act. Teachers must be certified by the state or working toward certification.	Teachers in private schools may not be required to have certification; instead they are having expertise with a undergraduate or graduate degree in the subject they teach.
Students	The children in most public schools reflect the community. In many public schools, there is a diversity of students.	The student's population at private schools is determined through a selection process; all students must apply and be accepted in order to attend. Although students may be from different neighborhoods, they will probably have similar goals and interest.
Class Size	Many states recognize the value of small classes and try to keep class small in grade K-3. As students move from elementary school to middle and high school the class size get larger especially in large school district and urban schools.	Private schools are generally committed to providing small classes and individual attention to students. Many parents choose private schools for this reason.

Special Needs	Due to special education laws, public schools must educate all children, and provide the necessary programs to meet their special needs. If a student has an IEP or a 504 plan it is the law that the school make sure that the students with particular needs are met. Public schools have special education programs and teachers who are trained to work with students with special needs.	Private schools do not have to accept children with special needs, and many choose not to and as a result most private school do not have special education programs or teachers trained to work with students with special needs. Private schools will try to help all the students they admit, but extra resources may also come at an additional cost.

The Public Schools vs. Private Schools is an ongoing debate. Private schools students typically score higher than public school students on standardized tests but a study by the National Center for Education Statistics released in 2006 that took into account student's background told a different story. Public schools student in the fourth and eighth grade scored almost as well or better in reading and math except that private school students excelled in eight grade reading. Earlier in 2006, an analysis of math scores by the University of Illinois researchers found similar results to t he National Center for Education study. The debate over which schools does a better job is far from over but when researchers compare the schools they must taking into account that private school serve the more advantaged populations, and public school serve the advantage, below advantage and students with special needs. There are a few fundamental differences between public and private schools, but the bottom line is there are great public schools and there are great private schools. The trick is to find the school that best fits your child's needs

Chapter 7
What Parents Needs To Know About
The NCAA Rules

Eligibility Standrads Reference Sheet

This information is provided from the following website: www.ncaa.org
For more information you can visited the clearinghouse Web site at:
www.ncaaclearninghouse.net

KNOW THE RULES:

CORE -COURSES

● Starting August 1, 2008, **16 core courses** will be required for **NCAA Division I only**. This rule applies to any student entering any Division I college or university on or after August 1, 2008.

● **14 core courses are required in NCAA Division II.**

Division I	Division II
16 Core- Course Rule	14 Core- Course Rule
● 4 years of English	● 3 years of English
● 3 years of mathematics (Algebra I or higher	● 2 years of mathematics (Algebra I or higher)
● 2 years of natural/physical science (1 year of lab if offered by high school	● 2 years of natural/physical science (1 year of lab if offered by high school)
● 1 year of additional English, mathematics or natural/physical science	● 2 years of additional English, mathematics or natural/physical
● 2 years of social science	● 2 years of additional English, mathematics or natural/physical science
● 4 years of additional courses (from any areas above, foreign language or non-doctrine religion/philosophy)	● 2 years of social science
	● 3 years of additional courses (from any area above, foreign language or non-doctrine religion/ philosophy).

TEST SCORES

{ **Division I** has a sliding scale for test scores and grade-point average. The sliding for those requirements is show on the next page.

●**Division II** has a minimum SAT score requirement of 820 or an ACT sun score of 68.

●The SAT score used for NCAA purposes includes **only** the critical reading and math sections. **The writing section of the SAT is not used**.

●The ACT score used NCAA purposes is a sum of the four sections on the ACT: English, math, reading and science.

●ALL SAT and ACT scores must be reported directly to the NCAA Initial-Eligibility Clearinghouse by the testing agency. Test scores that appear on transcript will no longer be used. When registering for the SAT or ACT, use the clearinghouse code of 9999 to make sure the score is reported to the clearinghouse.

Grade-Point Average

● Only core courses are used in calculation the grade-point average

● **Be sure** to look at your high school's list of NCAA-approved core course on the clearinghouse Web Site to make certain that the courses being taken have been approved as core courses. The Web site is www.ncaaclearinghouse.net

●Division I grade-point average requirements are listed in the table below.

● The Division II grade-point-average requirement is a minimum 2.00.

NCAA DIVISION I SLIDING SCALE CORE GRADE-POINT AVERAGE TEST-SCORE NEW CORE GPA/TEST SCORE INDEX		
Core GPA	SAT verbal and math	ACT
3.550 & above	400	37
3.525	410	38
3.500	420	39
3.475	430	40
3.450	440	41
3.425	450	41
3.400	460	42
3.375	470	42
3.350	480	43
3.325	490	44
3.300	500	44
3.275	510	45
3.250	520	46

Core GPA	SAT Verbal and Math	ACT
3.225	530	46
3.200	540	47
3.175	550	47
3.150	560	48
Core GPA	SAT Verbal and Math	ACT
3.125	570	49
3.100	580	49
3.075	590	50
3.050	600	50
3.025	610	51
3.000	620	52
2.975	630	52
2.950	640	53
2.925	650	53
2.900	660	54
2.875	670	55
2.850	680	56
2.825	690	56
2.800	700	57
2.775	710	58
2.750	720	59
2.725	730	59
2.700	730	60
2.675	740-750	61
2.650	760	62
2.625	770	63
2.600	780	74
2.575	790	65
2.550	800	66
2.525	810	67
2.500	820	68
2.475	830	69
2.450	840-850	70
2.425	860	70
2.400	860	71
2.375	870	72
2.350	880	73.

Core GPA	SAT Verbal and Math	ACT
2.325	890	74
2.300	900	75
2.275	910	76
Core GPA	SAT Verbal and Math	ACT
2.250	920	77
2.225	930	78
2.200	940	79
2.175	950	80
2.150	960	80
2.125	960	81
2.100	970	82
2.075	980	83
2.050	990	84
2.025	1000	85
2.000	1010	86

While you are thinking about your child future, don't forget to pay attention to the present. As parents you should reassure, encourage and support. Together you and your child can learn during high school what the requirements for graduation, what preparation courses are recommendation for college, and how they should structure their high school years to prepare for college. When helping your child plan for college while they are in high school there are the several key areas to consider: courses, standardized tests, extra curricular activities, community service, letter for recommendations for college and financial aid for college. Start researching financial aid in the ninth grade and familiarize your child with requirements and deadlines, so they will be prepared to apply for college. The guides have been written to give parents the opportunity to have a better understand of the laws that governs the public school in the United States.

CHAPTER 8
Forms

Goal- Setting Form

Date _____

Long-Range Goal _____

_____

_____

_____

_____

_____

_____

_____

_____

_____

_____

_____

Short –Range Goal _____

_____

_____

_____

_____

_____

_____

Student: Thing I will do to begin reaching my goal:

_____

_____

_____

_____

_____

_____

_____

_____

_____

Signature :

Parents _____

Student:_____

Letter to Teacher re: Homework Assignments

Sample Letter

Dear, (Teacher Name)

We are currently working with (Child Name) on an assignments plan for (Child Name) to complete assignments. We need your help with this plan. At the beginning of each class period (Child Name) will give you the Assignment Record to determine if (Child Name) has completely: Class work Tests, Homework by due dates. If (Child Name) has met his/her or her responsibilities, please initial the daily progress report. If you are willing to assist us in this effort, please sign the attached contract, your cooperation and time is invaluable and will be appreciated.

ASSIGNMENTS RECORD				
Student_____ Subject_____ Teacher _____ Period_____				
	Date due	Date completed	Possible points	Points Earned
Monday In class assignments				
Test				
Homework				
Quizzes				
Tuesday				
In class assignments				
Tests				
Homework Quizzes				
Wednesday				
In class assignments Test				
Homework				
Quizzes				
Thursday				
In class assignments Test				
Homework				
Quizzes				

Friday				
In class assignments				
Homework				
Tests				
Quizzes				

If there is nothing to record for the day, please initial in the space next to the appropriate date anyway. Thank for your cooperation

ESATABLISHED HOMEWROK ROUTINES

Time (PM)	Mon	Tue	Wed	Thru	Fri	Sat	Sun
4:00							
4:30							
5:00							
5:30							
6:00							
6:30							
7:00							
7:30							
8:00							
9:30							
10:00							
10:30							
11:00							

If your child has difficulty with time management or carrying out responsibilities and need to learn better self discipline, you might help to select a set time for during homework, for example your child could study math each day at 4:00- 4:30. If the student has no homework in that class, they should still review over the class notes. A consistent routine means that each week the student study habits should improve. If the student is working on one assignment, help the students to learn how to pace themselves. Make sure the student know the policy about turning in late homework or assignments.

REFERENCE

Andrew, W., Chitwood, S., & Hayden, D. (1997). Negotiating the special education maze: A guide for parents and teachers. (3rd Ed.) Bethesda, MD: Woodbine House.

Armstrong, T. (2000). Multiple intelligence in the classroom. 2nd edition. Association for Supervision and Curriculum Development. Alexandria, VA.

Barone, C., Aguirre-Deandreis, A. I., & Trickett, E. J. (1991). Mean-ends problem-solving skills, life stress, and social support as mediators of adjustment in the normative transition to high school. AMERICAN JOURNAL OF COMMUNITY PSYCHOLOGY 19(2). 207-225

Bateman, D. &Bateman, C.F. (2001). A principal's guide to special education. Council for Exceptional Children. Arlington, Virginia.

Bateman, B.D. & Linden, M.A. (1998). Better IEPs: How to develop legally correct and educationally useful programs (3rd Ed.). Longmont, CO: Sopris West

Barton, P.E.(2004, November). Why does the gap persist? *Educational Leadership, 62, (3),* 8-13.

Bush, G.W. (2002). Fact Sheet: No Child left Behind Act. The White House Newsletter. Retrieved February 27, 2007 from, from http://www.whitehouse.gov/news/release/2002/01/20020108.html.

Cortiella, C. (2008). IDEA Close Up: Disciplining Students with Disabilities. Retrieved June 15, 2008 from http://www.schwqblearning.org/articles.aspx?r=1126

Council for Exceptional Children. (1999). The IEP team guide. Arlington, Va.

Cutler, B.C. (1995). *You, your child and "special education: A guide to making the system work.* Baltimore, MD: Paul H. Brookes.

Department of Education. http://www.ed.gov.index.index.html.

Department of Education. National Center for Educational Statistics. Digest of Education Statistics (2004). Database, 2007, Pearson Education, Inc.

Dougherty, C.(2002,September). States must improve data for adequate yearly progress. Retrieved December 15, 2006 from: http://www.ecs.org.

Drasgrow.E.J Yell, M.L. & Robinson, T.R.(2001, November/December). Developing legally correct and educationally appropriate IEPs. Remedial and Special Education, 22(6), 359-373.

DuFour, R., &DuFor, R. (2004, June). What ever it takes: How professional learning communities respond what kids don't know. Bloomington, IN: solution Tree

Dunn, R., & Dunn, K. (1992). *Teaching elementary students through their individual learning styles: Practical approaches* for grades 3-6. Boston: Allen & Bacon.

Dunn, R. & Geiser, W.F. (1998). Solving the homework problem: A heart-to-heart versus a tongue-in-check approach. Michigan Principal, 74(3), 7-10.

Educational and Secondary act of 1965. Retrieved March 24, 2008, from http://www.si.unm.edy/si2006/SUSAN_A/TIMELINE/TIM_0015.HTH.

Education Trust. (2003). African American achievement in America Education Trust. Retrieved December 15, 2006 from www.edtrust.org.

Education Trust (2008). Too many states consistently spend less money in school districts educating English Language Learners, Low-income students and students of color. Retrieved April 28, 2008 from www.edtrust.org.

Families and Advocates Partnership for Education (FAPE). (2001). *Planning your child's individualized education program* (IEP): Retrieved April 28, 2008 from www.fape.org.

Giangreco, M.F., Cloninger, C.J., & Iverson (1998).*Choosing outcomes and accommodations for children (COACH): A guide to educational planning for students with disabilities* (2nd ed.). Baltimore, MD: Paul H. Broookes.

Gibbs, G.S. & Dyches, T.T. (2000). Guide to writing quality individualized education programs: *What's best for students with disabilities?* Needham Heights, MA: Allyn & Bacon.

Good, T.L., & Brophy, J.E. (2003). *Looking in classrooms* (9th ed). Boston: Allyn and Bacon.

Gulton, G. & Oakes, J. (1995). Opporutnity to learn and conceptions of educational Equality. *Educational Evaluation and Policy analysis*, 17(3), 323-336.

Gutek, G. (2004). Educational philosophy and changes. Boston, MA: Pearson Custom Publishing.

Hertzog. C.J., Morgan, P.L., Diamond, P.A., & Walker, M.J. (1996). Transition to high school: A look at student perceptional, Becoming, 7(2), 6-8.

Historical Facts about the American Education System. http://www.pbs.org/merrow/tv/trust/index.html. http://www.ed.gov
IDEA (2004). http://idea.ed.gov.

IDEA Local Implementation by Local Administrators. *A guide for Prinicples Implementing IDEA*. Council for Exceptional Children, Arlington Va.

Lecker, W. (2005). The Promise and Challenges of the "No Child Left Behind Act." Access-NO Child Left Behind Act. Retrieved December 26, 2005 from http://www.schoolfunding.info/federal/NCLB/nclb_brief.phps.

Maryland Department of Education (2002). The Bridges to Excellences in Public Schools Act of 2002. Retrieved February 10, 2007, from http://marylandpublicschools.org?MSDE/curriculum/.

Mathematics Voluntary State Curriculum (2003.August). Teaching and learning mathematics Maryland Department of Education, Retrieved November 30, 2006 from http://www.mdk12.org/instructional/curriculum/mathematics/index.html.

National Center for Education Statistics Government Database of Education Statistics. www.nces.ed.gov.

NAEP: State Profiles. *National Center for Education Statistics*. Retrieved December 15, 2005, from http://nces.eds.gov/nationsreportcard/state/profile.

National Center for Learning Disabilities. No child left behind: Determining appropriate assessment accommodations for students with disabilities. Retrieved March 24, 2008 from www.LD.org

National Commission of Mathematics 21 Century. (2001). Before it's to late. Retrieved June 15, 2006, from http://www.ed.gov/inita/Math/glenn/report.pdf.

National Council of Teachers of English. http://www.ncte.org/

National Council of Teachers of Mathematics (2000). *Principles and standards for* school mathematics. Reston, VA. NCTM.

National Council of Teachers of Mathematics. (1998). *Principles and standards for school mathematics*. Reston, VA: NCTM.

National Council for the Social Studies. http://www.ncss.org/

National Education Association (NEA) (2004). Horizon of Opportunities celebrating 50 years of Brown v. Board of Education May 17, 1954-2004. Retrieved May 17, 2004, from http://www.nea.org/brownvboard/index2.html.

National Science Teachers Association-Science & Education. http://www.nsta,org/

NCAA FRESHMAN-ELIGIBILITY STANDRADS QUICK REFERENCE SHEET. www. ncaa.org or www.ncaaclearninghouse.net.

Office of Special Education and Rehabilitative Service (OSERS). U.S. Department of Education (2000). A guide to the individualized education program. Washington D.C. Retrieved March 24, 2008 from www.ed.gov/parents/needs/speced/iepguide/index.html

Phelan, P., Yu, H.C., & Davidson, A.L.(1994). *Navigating the psychosocial pressure of adolescence: The voices and experiences of high school youth.* AMERICAN EDUCATIONAL RESEARCH JOURNAL, 31(2). 415-447.

Price, Mayfied. McFadden & Marsh (2001) *Chapter 6, Accommodations Strategies Special Education for Inclusive Classrooms.* Retrieved December 26, 2005 from http://www. parrotpublishing.com/Inclusion_Chapter_6.htm

Schugurensky, D. (1965). Selected moments of the 20th century. *History of Education*: Selected Moments. Retrieved December 15, 2005, from http://ww

Siegel, L, M. (2001). The complete IEP guide: How to advocate for your special ed. child (2nd, ed). Berkeley. CA: Nolo Press.

Special Education Inclusion. (2001). *Teaching and Learning.* Retrieved October 28, 2005, from http://www.weC.ORG/RESOURCE/JUNE96/SPECED.HTM

Special Education and the Individuals with Disabilities Education Act. (2004). NEA-Issues in Education. Retrieved December 26, 2005 from http://www.nea.org/specialed/index.html

Thurlow, M, PhD. (2004). Assessment: A Key Component of Education Reform.
Learning Disabilities on line. Retrieved December 26, 2005, from http://www.Idonline.org/ Id_indepth/special_edeucation/thurlow-assessment.html

Vars, G.F., (1998). "You've come a long, way, baby" In R.David (ed.), MOVING FORWARD FROM THE PAST: EARLY WRITING AND CURRENT REFLECTIONS OF MIDDLE SCHOOL FOUNDERS (pp.222-233). Columbus, OH: National Middle School Association; Pittsburgh: Pennsylvania Middle School Association.

Virginia State Department of Education. Standards of Learning Currently in Effect for Virginia Public School. http://www.doe.virginia.gov/

U.S. Department of Education. (2004). IDEA'97 Provisions on General Assessment in Final Regs. General State and District-wide Assessments-Topic Brief.

Retrieved December 26, 2005 from http://www.ed.gov/policy/speced/leg/idea/breif2.html. U.S. Department of Education (2003) Paige approve Maryland state accountability plan

Under No Child Left Behind. Retrieved December 15, 2005, from
   http://www.ed.gov/news/pressreleases

United Sates Department of Education (2002). *No child left behind.* Retrieved December 6, 2006, from http://www.ed.gov/nclb.overview/intro/exexsumm.html

United State Department of Education (2002). *Title I- Improving the Academic Achievement of The Disadvantaged.* Retrieved March 24, 2008 from http://www.ed.gov/policy/elsec/leg/esea02/pg1.html

United State Department of Education (2007). *Major sections of No Child Left Behind Act.* Retrieved April 21, 2008 http://answers.ed.gov/cgi=bin/education.cfg/php/enduser/std_adp.php?p_faqid=99&p_creat..

Wright P.W.D., & Pamela D. (2000).*Your Child's IEP: Practical and Legal Guidance for Parents.* Retreived June 15, 2008 from http://user.cybrzn.com/kenyonck/add/iep_guidance.html